The Second Logo Book
Advanced Techniques in Logo

The Second Logo Book
Advanced Techniques in Logo

Dan Weston

Scott, Foresman and Company
Glenview, Illinois   London

ISBN 0-673-18079-4

Copyright © 1985 Scott, Foresman and Company.
All Rights Reserved.
Printed in the United States of America.

Library of Congress Cataloging in Publication Data

Weston, Dan.
   The second logo book.

   Bibliography: p. 203
   Includes index.
   1. LOGO (Computer program language)   2. Computer
graphics.   I. Title.
QA76.73.L63W47   1985   001.64′24   85-1883
ISBN 0-673-18079-4

1   2   3   4   5   6—KPF—90   89   88   87   86   85

Notice of Liability

**To my father,
who showed me how to build things**

Acknowledgments

I am deeply indebted to the members of the research staff of Logo Computer Systems, Inc. for introducing me to Logo, allowing me to learn by my own exploration, and answering my questions when I got stuck. They displayed unusual generosity when they took me, literally a stranger off the street, into their midst during the hectic months when they were putting the finishing touches on their version of Logo for the Apple II. In this book I attempt to express in my own way many ideas that I first encountered at Logo Computer Systems, Inc. The good parts of this book stem from my apprenticeship there. Any parts that fall short reflect my own shortcomings.

I am also grateful for conversations and recursive discussions with Tim Riordon. Werner Brandt supplied logistic support and friendship. Stan Krute provided Saturday morning telephone conversation and shared a world view. Many thanks to all the students and teachers of Logo who asked, "What else can we do with Logo?"

My wife Leslie gave encouragement and criticism and gave up most of our free time together while I was writing this book. Finally, thanks to my daughter Sarah for debugging the blocks world.

Contents

INTRODUCTION

HOW TO USE THIS BOOK

Who Should Read This Book

This book is intended for you if you already have some familiarity with Logo. It is written to extend the range of your expectations of what Logo can do. Although it is assumed that you can use the Logo system and editor to define and modify simple Logo procedures, you can use this book with a minimal amount of previous experience with Logo. This book is for you if you are eager to explore ideas and learn elegant problem-solving skills with a computer. The book promotes hands-on learning. You will benefit from working with Logo on a computer as you read along, but that is not absolutely necessary.

What This Book Covers

Chapter 1 is an introduction to turtle graphics; it also discusses the definition of procedures and the use of inputs. It is fairly elementary and can be used by anyone with some knowledge of Logo.

Chapter 2 introduces recursion with a series of recursive graphics projects. It lays the basis for the understanding of recursion that is reinforced by projects in later chapters.

Chapter 3 is an introduction to list processing with Logo. This chapter assumes that the reader knows nothing about this aspect of Logo. It introduces fundamental concepts and gives practice with applications.

Chapter 4 develops a set of recursive tools that operate on lists. It illustrates key recursive strategies and puts the **OUTPUT** primitive to extensive use.

Chapter 5 introduces property lists and uses them to create the blocks world. This chapter assumes that you know nothing about property lists.

Chapter 6 explores the recursive wonders of trees. It draws trees and then creates abstract trees to hold data. It is recommended that you read chapter 2 before you read about trees, because chapter 6 assumes that you are familiar with the mechanisms of recursion.

Chapter 7 develops procedures for pattern matching and then applies them to a data-base system. This chapter demonstrates Logo's practicality.

You can tackle most of the chapters on their own, without having read previous chapters, except as noted above.

Appendix A is a collection of generalizations about fundamental Logo topics. It is most useful as a reference. Logo is designed so that learning proceeds from the concrete, experiential level to the abstract. Throughout the body of the book, generalizations are drawn from the particulars of the projects at hand. Appendix A is a collection of these abstract generalizations.

The subject of Appendix B is workspace management. Appendix C explains how to add property lists to Terrapin Logo. Appendixes D and E are a list of relevant books and articles and a glossary of selected Logo primitives.

What This Book Doesn't Cover

Many interesting Logo projects are not included here because they use features (such as the capability to produce music or other kinds of sound) that are particular to one Logo version or another. However, the concepts developed in the projects in this book can be applied in many other areas. You are encouraged to explore the capabilities of your own system and to formulate your own projects.

Also, this book does not cover fundamental Logo system operation because such topics as the editor and disk storage are handled adequately by user manuals and other introductory books.

Finally, this book does not begin to cover the range of topics that lend themselves to exploration via Logo. The more you use Logo, the more areas of inquiry seem to present themselves for investigation. The Logo universe is a particularly rich one. I hope the projects presented in this book help you think of your own projects and further your own Logo education.

NOTES ON DIFFERENT VERSIONS OF LOGO

The Logo procedures listed in this book are written in Dr. Logo from Digital Research. You can run the procedures as written, on the IBM PC or PCjr using Dr. Logo, or on the Apple II, IIe, or IIc using Apple Logo. Dr. Logo users must note, however, that the program listings have been typeset in uppercase characters even though Dr. Logo expects all primitives and key words to be lowercase. The projects here do not involve extensions to Logo that are particular to any one computer. They should therefore work with any version of Logo that approximates Apple Logo.

Dr. Logo was chosen because, while it follows very closely the standards set by Apple Logo with regard to primitive names and syntax, Dr. Logo's format for procedure definitions is more flexible. Apple Logo and others require that you type a procedure, or primitive, and its inputs together on one logical line, that is, without using the <return> key. Dr. Logo, on the other hand, allows you to position parts of an expression on successive lines. Thus, a procedure that looks like this in Apple Logo:

```
TO DEMO :INPUT
IF :INPUT = "ACHOO [PRINT [BLESS YOU]] [PRI!
 NT [YOU SEEM HEALTHY ENOUGH]]
END
```

or like this in Terrapin Logo:

```
TO DEMO :INPUT
IF :INPUT = "ACHOO THEN PRINT [BLESS YOU] EL!
 SE PRINT [YOU SEEM HEALTHY ENOUGH]
END
```

looks like this in Dr. Logo:

```
TO DEMO :INPUT
IF :INPUT = "ACHOO
     [PRINT [BLESS YOU]]
     [PRINT [YOU SEEM HEALTHY ENOUGH]]
END
```

(Note that an exclamation point (!) marks a break in a line that is too long to fit unbroken on the screen. Do not type the exclamation point or press the <return> key when you are typing in such a line; let the computer supply the line break automatically.)

In Dr. Logo the then and else inputs to the **IF** expression can be put on separate lines, as long as the then and else lines begin with a space or a tab.

Other examples of this type of formatting can be seen with primitives or procedures that take more than one input the way the **IF** command does. So in Apple Logo you use this format:

```
PPROP "JIM "FAVORITE.SONG [BIG EYED BEANS!
 FROM VENUS]
```

but in Dr. Logo you can use this format:

```
PPROP "JIM
       "FAVORITE.SONG
       [BIG EYED BEANS FROM VENUS]
```

The advantages of Dr. Logo's format are especially clear when the inputs to the procedure or primitive are themselves the outputs of other procedures. Compare Apple Logo and Terrapin Logo's

```
PRINT FPUT "ONCE BUTFIRST [NEVER IN MY LIFE]
```

with Dr. Logo's

```
PRINT FPUT "ONCE
           BUTFIRST [NEVER IN MY LIFE]
```

In this book I have adopted the convention of matching beginning and ending parentheses by placing the closing parenthesis one column to the right of the opening parenthesis whenever they are not on the same line. This is similar to the way that many people format programs in C. Compare Apple Logo and Terrapin Logo's

```
PRINT (SENTENCE "THE [QUICK BROWN] LAST [RED!
 FOX] [JUMPED OVER] "THE (FPUT "LAZY [DOG]))
```

with Dr. Logo's

```
PRINT (SENTENCE "THE
               [QUICK BROWN]
               LAST [RED FOX]
               [JUMPED OVER]
               "THE
               (FPUT "LAZY [DOG])
        )    ; END SENTENCE
```

This format can also be used with logical operators that can take a variable number of inputs. Compare Apple Logo's

```
IF (OR :WIDTH > 35 :LENGTH > 40 :DEPTH > !
 70) [PRINT [TOO BIG]]
```

and Terrapin Logo's

```
IF (ANYOF :WIDTH > 35 :LENGTH > 40 :DEPTH > !
 70) THEN PRINT [TOO BIG]
```

with Dr. Logo's

```
IF (OR :WIDTH > 35
       :LENGTH > 40
       :DEPTH > 70
    )    ; END OR
   [PRINT [TOO BIG]]
```

The advantages of the free format are easy to see in a case like this.

Note the use of the semicolon to mark a comment. The inclusion of comments is, of course, optional. I make liberal use of comments in the procedures in this book. Although it is easier to write self-explanatory code in Logo than it is in some other languages, it is still a good idea to use comments in your own procedures. Check to see how your version of Logo handles them. Apple Logo, for instance, does not allow comments unless you define your own comment procedure, such as

```
TO ; :COMMENT
END
```

Your comment has to be enclosed in brackets, like this:

```
TO FOO
; [THIS PROGRAM DOES VERY LITTLE]
PRINT "FOO
END
```

Opening and closing brackets are positioned in the same way as parentheses. The arrangement is helpful when you use complex procedures with **IF** statements requiring that the then and else inputs be enclosed in brackets. Let's return to our original example and modify it to illustrate. Compare Apple Logo's

```
TO DEMO :INPUT
IF :INPUT = "ACHOO [PRINT [BLESS YOU] PRINT !
 [HOPE YOU FEEL BETTER] PRINT [TAKE CARE]]  !
 [PRINT [YOU SEEM HEALTHY ENOUGH]]
END
```

and Terrapin Logo's

```
TO DEMO :INPUT
IF :INPUT = "ACHOO THEN PRINT [BLESS YOU]  !
 PRINT [HOPE YOU FEEL BETTER] PRINT [TAKE C!
 ARE] ELSE PRINT [YOU SEEM HEALTHY ENOUGH]
END
```

with Dr. Logo's

```
TO DEMO :INPUT
IF :INPUT = "ACHOO
    [PRINT [BLESS YOU]
     PRINT [HOPE YOU FEEL BETTER]
     PRINT [TAKE CARE]
     ]   ; END THEN
   ; ELSE
    [PRINT [YOU SEEM HEALTHY ENOUGH]]
END
```

In general, if you are not using Dr. Logo or some other version that allows free formatting, you must place lines shown indented in this book together on one line with the unindented line above them. I think you will find that the format of the listings in this book helps you understand the structure and flow of the procedures. I also think you will find that converting the format is easy if you refer to the examples above. The syntax and commands are exactly the same for Dr. Logo and Apple Logo in all the examples in this book, so conversion requires only that you keep the formatting conventions in mind.

1 TURTLE GRAPHICS

THE FUNDAMENTALS ⎯⎯⎯⎯⎯⎯⎯⎯⎯⎯⎯⎯⎯⎯⎯⎯⎯⎯⎯

Turtle graphics is a system of computer drawing that allows the user to control an imaginary animal that lives on the plane of the video monitor. This animal can turn, move forward and back, and draw lines to trace its path around the screen. Actually, the earliest turtle graphics systems were built around small robots that moved on the floor and had real pens that could draw on large sheets of paper. It was only later that these robots, called *turtles*, could be represented on a graphics monitor.

Turtle graphics is not unique to Logo. Many other computer languages have incorporated turtle graphics. There is much more to Logo than just turtle graphics, as the later chapters show, but graphics is fun and easy to understand, so this is a good place to start.

The first command that you can give the turtle is **CLEARSCREEN** (abbreviated **CS**). That command places the turtle, represented by a small triangle, at the center of your screen, facing upward. At this point you can direct the turtle to go **FORWARD** (**FD**), **BACK** (**BK**), **RIGHT** (**RT**), or **LEFT** (**LT**). With **FORWARD** and **BACK**, you must tell the turtle how many steps to move, as in

```
FORWARD 30
BACK 50
FORWARD 91
```

For **RIGHT** and **LEFT**, you must give the number of degrees for the turtle to turn. These commands actually only make the turtle pivot on one spot; they do not move the turtle from its location. Try these out with

```
RIGHT 45
LEFT 90
RIGHT 193
```

You should be able to see the turtle turn with each command. This kind of immediate feedback to a command was one of the original goals of the Logo designers, and it provides a visual verification that the command has been carried out. Seeing the turtle turn also shows you in which direction the next **FORWARD** or **BACK** command will move the turtle. Take some time now to drive the turtle around the screen with combinations of these four commands. If you decide that you would like to start with a clean slate, type in **CLEARSCREEN**.

On most microcomputer versions of Logo, the graphics resolution limits the turtle to 100 to 150 steps in any direction from the center of the screen before it goes off the edge of the screen. Experiment with your particular version to see how many steps there are to the edges.

You can give any one of three commands that change the way the turtle behaves when it reaches the edge of the screen. If you type **WRAP**, then when the turtle reaches one edge of the screen it wraps around and appears on the opposite edge. (This is the default mode in Apple Logo.) In **WRAP** mode, you can get interesting effects by typing

```
CLEARSCREEN RT 15 FORWARD 10000
```

(Note that it is okay to type more than one command on a line as long as the commands are separated by spaces.)

Another command that affects the turtle's behavior at the screen edge is **WINDOW**. When **WINDOW** is in effect, the turtle continues off the edge of the screen without wrapping. This is the default mode in Dr. Logo. You cannot see the turtle, but it is still responding to your commands although it is outside the visual field. If you try to go too far beyond the edge, Logo tells you:

```
TURTLE OUT OF BOUNDS
```

The exact distance at which this happens differs for each version of Logo. Experiment with your turtle to see how far you can push it.

The third command regarding the screen edge is **FENCE**. When this is in effect, the turtle stops at the edge of the screen and gives the message

```
TURTLE OUT OF BOUNDS
```

It isn't actually necessary to specify what happens when the turtle reaches the edge because all versions of Logo pick one of these three options by default, depending on the version. You need to be concerned only if you want something other than the default.

Now you know enough to drive the turtle around the screen and draw some pictures. Spend some time doing just these things so that you are comfortable with the turtle commands covered so far. Two additional commands that you should know at this point are **PENUP** and **PENDOWN**. When the **PENDOWN** command is in effect (the default mode), the turtle draws a line tracing its path over the screen. When you give the command **PENUP**, the turtle stops drawing lines until you issue another **PENDOWN** command. This allows you to move the turtle to a position on the screen without drawing a line and then to put the pen down to begin drawing. Try out these commands by making the turtle draw your initials on the screen.

DEFINING PROCEDURES

So far in this chapter we have been using the turtle graphics commands only in the *immediate* mode. That is, you type in one or more commands on a line, you hit <return>, and then the turtle responds accordingly. This kind of immediate feedback helps you learn the commands and get accustomed to the system. The drawback is that if you type in a long series of commands that create a design you particularly like, then you must type in the entire series again if you want to see the design again.

As described in Appendix A, Logo allows you to define procedures that take a series of Logo commands that could be typed in from the keyboard and group them together under one name. For instance, if you want to draw a box, you can define the following procedure:

```
TO BOX
FORWARD 70
RIGHT 90
FORWARD 70
RIGHT 90
FORWARD 70
RIGHT 90
FORWARD 70
END
```

Now if you want to draw this box on the screen, you need type in only the word **BOX** rather than the entire series of commands. By defining a procedure called **BOX**, you have taught the computer a new word that it understands in much the same way as it understands **FORWARD** or **CLEARSCREEN**.

You can now define another procedure using **BOX**, such as

```
TO FOURSQUARE
BOX
BOX
BOX
BOX
END
```

This procedure uses a previously defined procedure as part of its definition. This is the secret to the power of Logo: you can combine and build procedures from the simple level up to the more complex.

Note that this procedure takes advantage of the fact that in the original **BOX**, the turtle makes only three 90-degree turns. This leaves it facing in a different direction than when it started drawing the box. In Logo, we say that its *heading* is different. As you go on through the projects in this book, you will see that it is often very important to make sure that the turtle is returned to its original state, both in position and heading, when it finishes a procedure.

The procedure **BOX** can also include the **REPEAT** command. As explained in Appendix A, **REPEAT** needs two inputs: the number of times to repeat and a list of actions to repeat. The list of actions is enclosed in square brackets:

```
TO BOX2
REPEAT 4 [FORWARD 70 RIGHT 90]
END
```

This procedure is slightly different from the original in that it has four 90-degree turns rather than three and thus returns the turtle to its original position and heading.

The list of actions enclosed in the brackets may be anything that you could normally type into Logo and expect it to understand.

Now that we have a procedure to draw a box, we can define another procedure to draw it many times, turning the turtle slightly after each box. This is called *spinning*, and the procedure looks like this:

```
TO SPINBOX
REPEAT 36 [BOX2 RT 10]
END
```

Figure 1.1 shows the result of **SPINBOX**.

Sometimes you can take a figure that in itself is not very interesting and spin it to get rather dramatic effects. Try this out yourself by defining your own figures and then substituting them into **SPINBOX** in the place of **BOX2**.

USING INPUTS

Knowing that the turtle must turn a total of 360 degrees to come full circle to its original heading, we can use other combinations of repetition and turning to get different spin pictures. Try these options:

```
REPEAT 12 [BOX2 RT 30]
REPEAT 10 [BOX2 RT 36]
REPEAT 9 [BOX2 RT 40]
REPEAT 4 [BOX2 RT 90]
```

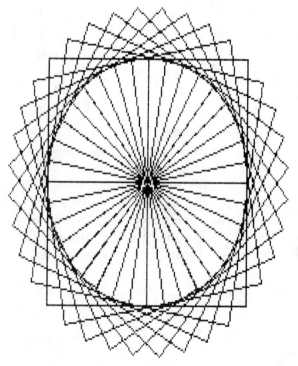

Figure 1.1
SPINBOX

From these examples, we can extract the generalization that the extra turn must be equal to 360 degrees divided by the number of repetitions. With Logo, this generalization can be encoded into the procedure in the form of an input, called **:HOWMANY**, that tells the procedure how many times to repeat and, indirectly, how much to turn after each box. The procedure looks like this:

```
TO SPINBOX2 :HOWMANY
REPEAT :HOWMANY [BOX2 RT 360 / :HOWMANY]
END
```

You define the input on the title line by placing **:HOWMANY** right next to **TO SPINBOX**. This tells the Logo interpreter that it should expect to see a number typed in next to **SPINBOX** whenever you use the procedure. Putting **:HOWMANY** on the title line reserves space for the input number. You give the number not when you are defining the procedure but only later when you are using the procedure. When defining the procedure, you use the colon notation, called *dots*, to tell Logo to watch out for a value that will be supplied later. To use this procedure, you must give it an input number, as in these examples. (You may want to use **CLEARSCREEN** between each example.)

```
SPINBOX2 12
SPINBOX2 10
SPINBOX2 36
SPINBOX2 90
```

This procedure shows how Logo can use inputs to a procedure to make the procedure more flexible. In this procedure, the input value **:HOWMANY** is used twice: once to determine the number of repetitions and a second time to calculate the degrees of turn required to spin the figure. The number that you type in next to **SPINBOX** when you use it is substituted wherever **:HOWMANY** appears in the procedure. Think of **:HOWMANY** as an empty container that is waiting to be filled with a number every time you use **SPINBOX**.

Carrying this idea of inputs further, we can go back to our procedure that draws the box and give it an input:

```
TO BOX3 :SIZE
REPEAT 4 [FORWARD :SIZE RT 90]
END
```

With this procedure you can draw boxes of any size by giving a number as input when using the procedure, as shown below:

```
BOX3 10
BOX3 20
BOX3 100
BOX3 44
```

Now we can combine this new, flexible box procedure with the spinning procedure and get a procedure that spins boxes of any size, any number of times. This **NEWSPIN** procedure takes two inputs, **:SIZE** and **:HOWMANY**:

```
TO NEWSPIN :SIZE :HOWMANY
REPEAT :HOWMANY [BOX3 :SIZE RT 360 / :HOWMANY]
END
```

To use it you type statements like these:

```
NEWSPIN 50 12      (figure 1.2)
NEWSPIN 80 4       (figure 1.3)
NEWSPIN 70 20      (figure 1.4)
NEWSPIN 50 6       (figure 1.5)
```

The first number that you give as input determines the size of the boxes, and the second number determines how many boxes are drawn around the circle.

You may find that you want to spend more time working with the turtle in the immediate mode before defining procedures. This is fine. You should move ahead only when you feel comfortable with the level at which you have been working. Once you can define simple procedures like **BOX** and **BOX2** using absolute values, then you will probably want to modify them to take inputs and become more flexible, as we have done here.

USING RANDOM NUMBERS ─────────────────

Once you can work with procedures that have inputs, you can use random inputs to introduce an element of unpredictability. Logo provides a primitive, **RANDOM**, that will produce random integers in a

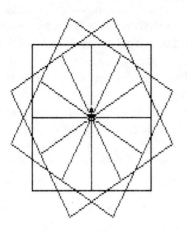

Figure 1.2
NEWSPIN 50 12

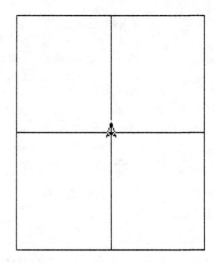

Figure 1.3
NEWSPIN 80 4

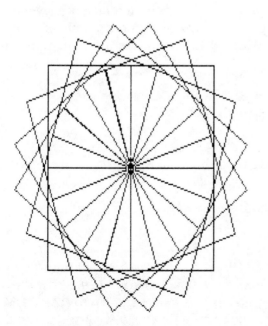

Figure 1.4
NEWSPIN 70 20

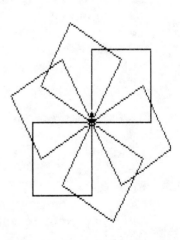

Figure 1.5
NEWSPIN 50 6

specified range. You must give **RANDOM** a number as input, and then it returns a random integer between 0 and 1 less than the number given as input. For instance, **RANDOM 10** outputs a number between 0 and 9, inclusive. If you want to get a number between 1 and 10, you can use **(RANDOM 10) + 1**. Adding 1 to the output of **RANDOM** is a way to avoid getting 0 as output.

To give you an idea of the kind of output you can expect from **RANDOM**, we can write a short procedure to repeatedly print random numbers on the screen:

```
TO RANDOMTEST
REPEAT 24 [PRINT RANDOM 10]
END
```

Now if you type **RANDOMTEST**, you get a list of twenty-four random numbers between 0 and 9.

If you want to see what happens when you use a different number as input to **RANDOM**, you can go in and edit **RANDOMTEST** and change the number. This can get cumbersome if you want to try several different numbers in succession, although Logo's built-in full-screen editor makes it easier than it would be in most other computer languages. A better way to be able to see many different sets of random numbers is to change **RANDOMTEST** so that it has an input to determine the upper limit of random numbers:

```
TO RANDOMTEST2 :NUMBER
REPEAT 24 [PRINT RANDOM :NUMBER]
END
```

To use this procedure you type things like

```
RANDOMTEST2 100
RANDOMTEST2 1
RANDOMTEST2 50
```

This is one more example of how inputs can be used with Logo procedures to make the procedures more flexible. You can see how the original procedure was written with an actual number given to **RANDOM**. Once we could see that the procedure was doing what we wanted it to do, then we went back and substituted an input for the actual number without disturbing the overall structure of the procedure. You may find this strategy useful in your own Logo investigations.

This procedure also illustrates Logo's ability to define short *tool procedures* on the spot to help you learn the ins and outs of the language. You will find that writing little procedures like **RANDOMTEST** and **RANDOMTEST2** allows you to test out features of the language quickly and thoroughly. This kind of flexibility helps make the Logo world the wonderful learning environment that it is.

Now, if you go back to the preceding section and get the procedure that draws a box of any size, **BOX3**, you can use it with random numbers as input, as shown by

```
BOX3 RANDOM 100
BOX3 RANDOM 30
BOX3 RANDOM 75
```

Since **RANDOM** outputs its result, it can be used anywhere Logo expects to find a number. This is one of the key features of Logo: a procedure that outputs a number can be used wherever a number can be used. Likewise, procedures that output other kinds of information, such as words or lists, can be used wherever those other kinds of information are expected. In later chapters we shall exploit this capability extensively.

Now you can use random numbers to draw boxes of random size. You might also use random numbers to simulate a coin toss:

```
TO TOSS
IF RANDOM 2 = 1
     [OUTPUT "HEADS]
     ; ELSE
     [OUTPUT "TAILS]
END
```

Yet another use for random numbers is to make the turtle move drunkenly around the screen. Define the following procedure:

```
TO DRUNK
REPEAT 1000 [RT RANDOM 360 FD RANDOM 50]
END
```

This procedure works best when **WRAP** mode is in effect.

Other chapters in this book use random numbers from time to time to add a degree of unpredictability to their execution. In this next section, we shall use random numbers and the Cartesian coordinate system to draw randomly sized boxes at random spots on the screen.

COORDINATE GEOMETRY ───────────────────

Traditionally, computer graphics has depended on the use of a Cartesian coordinate system, in which lines and dots are plotted by reference to their coordinates relative to an *x* axis and a *y* axis. Turtle graphics frees the user from thinking in these terms, allowing the user instead to draw figures with a combination of moves and turns that are not tied to specific spots on the screen. Turtle graphics is, in fact, built upon a coordinate field, but the field is hidden from the user. The computer does all the calculations necessary to translate turtle graphics commands into instructions for plotting absolute coordinates.

Figure 1.6 shows the coordinate field that lies underneath the turtle graphics screen. The *x* axis is horizontal, and the *y* axis is vertical. The center of the screen has the coordinates **[0 0]**. The coordinates are always referred to in a list, with the *x* coordinate first and the *y* coordinate second. Figure 1.6 shows several points in the field, with their coordinates. You can see that to the left of center, *x* coordinates are negative, and that below center, *y* coordinates are negative.

The actual extent of the coordinate field is different for different versions of Logo. Most microcomputer versions have a *y* range of about 120 to −120 and an *x* range of 140 to −140. You should experiment with your version to determine the bounds of the screen. For the sake of simplicity and compatibility, in our sample procedures here we shall assume that both the *x* and *y* ranges are 100 to −100. You can modify these values to fit your particular version.

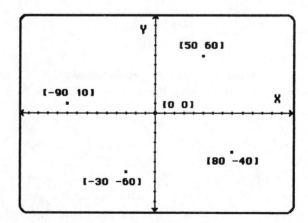

Figure 1.6
Turtle graphics coordinate field

To move the turtle to a specific point on the coordinate field, you can use the primitive **SETPOS**. This command takes a list of the *x* and *y* coordinates as input. It could be used as shown here:

```
SETPOS [100 0]
SETPOS [100 100]
SETPOS [-100 100]
SETPOS [-100 -100]
SETPOS [100 -100]
SETPOS [100 0]
```

Now we can combine random numbers with the coordinate field to draw boxes at random spots all over the screen. The procedure is easy once you figure out the trick for getting numbers in the 100 to −100 range. The expression **(RANDOM 201) − 100** gives the required range. The lowest number that **RANDOM 201** can give is 0, which gives −100 when you subtract 100. The highest number that **RANDOM 201** can give is 200, which gives 100 when you subtract 100.

The other trick that might not be obvious at first is to use the primitive **LIST** to put the output of the two calls to **(RANDOM 201) − 100** into a list. **SETPOS** requires that its input be in a list. You might think that you could write something like this:

```
SETPOS [(RANDOM 201) - 100 (RANDOM 201) - 100]
```

but that won't work because Logo does not go inside the brackets to execute the calls to **RANDOM**. You must have the procedure first evaluate **(RANDOM 201) − 100** twice and then feed the results to **LIST**, which puts the numbers into a list for **SETPOS**. (This is a rather subtle point, but an important one. **LIST** is discussed in depth in chapter 3.)

This method for using **RANDOM** to produce numbers between 100 and −100 can be packaged into a short Logo procedure so that you won't have to be concerned about the details in later procedures:

```
TO ANYPOINT
OUTPUT LIST (RANDOM 201) - 100 (RANDOM 201) - 100
END
```

Try it out now to see what kind of output you are getting:

```
REPEAT 24 [SHOW ANYPOINT]
```

We use the primitive **SHOW** rather than **PRINT** because **SHOW** does not strip the outer brackets off lists as **PRINT** does. You can see that the two numbers produced by **ANYPOINT** are put into a list before they are finally output. This way they are in the form that Logo expects for coordinates of a point on the turtle grid.

Now that we can produce random points in the coordinate field, we can write the procedure to place random-sized boxes at these points:

```
TO RANDOMBOXES
REPEAT 200 [PENUP
            SETPOS ANYPOINT
            PENDOWN
            BOX3 RANDOM 100
            ]   ; END REPEAT
END
```

These two procedures show how a problem can be broken into smaller parts in Logo. We were able to solve the random coordinates problem first and then package that solution in such a way that it could be used to help with the solution of the problem of the randomly placed boxes. Breaking a problem into manageable chunks is a key element in effective problem solving. Logo allows and encourages this strategy.

If you are working with a system that supports color, you might want to add a step to **RANDOMBOXES** that sets a random color number each time a new box is drawn. See the manual for the particular version you are using.

COMPUTER ETCH-A-SKETCH

In this section we shall develop a *one-finger environment* in which a user can control the turtle with one-letter commands. The system in some ways resembles an etch-a-sketch, a device that lets a person mechanically control the vertical and horizontal motion of a drawing instrument. With a computer, however, the user has more options.

This system needs a procedure that watches the keyboard, waits for the user to type in a letter, and then interprets that letter and takes the appropriate action. To begin with, let's assign actions to a few letters. Later you can make assignments of your own, as you learn how easy it is to modify the system.

F   move up one space
B   move down one space
R   move right one space
L   move left one space
U   pick the pen up
D   put the pen down
C   clear the screen
Q   quit

Rather than use turtle graphics commands to move the turtle, we shall use some new primitives that deal with the coordinate field. In the previous section, you saw how **SETPOS** can be used to move the turtle to an arbitrary point on the screen. In much the same way, **SETX** and **SETY** can be used to change either the x coordinate or the y coordinate alone. Two other primitives, **XCOR** and **YCOR**, output the current x coordinate and y coordinate, respectively. They can be combined to give effects like these:

Logo statement	*effect*
SETX XCOR + 1	move right one space
SETX XCOR − 1	move left one space
SETY YCOR + 1	move up one space
SETY YCOR − 1	move down one space

XCOR and **YCOR** are examples of Logo primitives that return information to the user about the state of the computer world rather than conveying information from the user to the computer. For almost every command that **SET**s something, like **SETPOS**, **SETX**, **SETHEADING**, and **SETPENCOLOR**, there is a corresponding primitive that tells you what the current value of that aspect of the system is, like **POS**, **XCOR**, **HEADING**, and **PENCOLOR**.

The final primitive we need for this project is **READCHAR**. This watches the keyboard and waits for the user to press a key; then it outputs the character that is pressed. **READCHAR** does not wait for the user to press the <return> key. The output of **READCHAR** is used by **MAKE** to assign the input character to a variable. In this procedure we make the variable "**CHAR** *local*. This means that its value is not known to all other procedures in the workspace. In general, it is not a good idea to create global variables unless there is some overriding reason to make them available to all procedures.

Now we can put all these elements together into the etch-a-sketch:

```
TO ETCH
LOCAL "CHAR    ; NOT A GLOBAL VARIABLE
MAKE "CHAR READCHAR
IF :CHAR = "F [SETY YCOR + 1]
IF :CHAR = "B [SETY YCOR - 1]
IF :CHAR = "R [SETX XCOR + 1]
IF :CHAR = "L [SETX XCOR - 1]
IF :CHAR = "U [PENUP]
IF :CHAR = "D [PENDOWN]
IF :CHAR = "C [CLEARSCREEN]
IF :CHAR = "Q [STOP]
ETCH
END
```

ETCH uses tail recursion to continually loop through its instruction cycle. It continues to take keyboard input until the user presses **Q**, at which point the procedure stops.

If you want to add more features, you can add more **IF :CHAR =** statements. Once the input character is assigned to the local variable **:CHAR**, the value of that variable, **:CHAR**, can be checked any number of times against possible values. This same strategy can be used with turtle graphics commands rather than coordinate field commands to give another sort of etch-a-sketch, but that project is left to you.

Certain keys can also be linked with user-defined procedures, so that, for example, pressing the **S** key draws a square and pressing the **T** draws a triangle. You might also want to add a help screen (available when the user presses **?**) that prints all the currently defined keys and their actions on the screen and then returns to the drawing in progress when the user presses <return>:

```
TO HELPSCREEN
TEXTSCREEN    ; SET TEXT MODE
CLEARTEXT
PRINT [KEYPRESS...ACTION]
PRINT [F..........MOVE FORWARD 1 SPACE]
PRINT [B..........MOVE BACK 1 SPACE]
PRINT [R..........MOVE RIGHT 1 SPACE]
PRINT [L..........MOVE LEFT 1 SPACE]
PRINT [U..........PENUP]
PRINT [D..........PENDOWN]
PRINT [C..........CLEARSCREEN]
PRINT [Q..........QUIT]
PRINT [?..........HELP]
PRINT []
PRINT []
PRINT [PRESS RETURN TO GO BACK TO PICTURE]
MAKE "GO.ON READLIST    ; WAIT FOR <RETURN>
SPLITSCREEN    ; RETURN TO GRAPHICS
END
```

This help screen can be added to **ETCH** with the line

```
IF :CHAR = "? [HELPSCREEN]
```

HELPSCREEN uses **TEXTSCREEN** and **CLEARTEXT** to clear the text screen in preparation for the printed help information. When the user decides to go back to the picture, **HELPSCREEN** uses **SPLITSCREEN** to set the screen for graphics with a four- or five-line text window at the bottom. Switching between text and graphics displays does not affect the contents of either one, so when the user returns to **SPLITSCREEN**, the user sees the image that was there at the time he or she asked for the help screen.

Finally, the line **MAKE "GO.ON READLIST** is just a way to make the procedure wait until the user presses the <return> key. **"GO.ON** is a dummy variable to which the output of **READLIST** is assigned. Another way of doing this same sort of thing—a way that is preferable because it does not create a global variable—is to feed **READLIST** into a procedure as an input and then do nothing with it:

```
TO DO.NOTHING :INPUT
END
```

If you use this procedure, then the line in **HELPSCREEN** that reads **MAKE "GO.ON READLIST** can be changed to

```
DO.NOTHING READLIST
```

The end result is the same, but the second method has the advantage of not producing an unnecessary global variable. As a good programmer, you want to create as few global variables as possible.

USING TRIGONOMETRY

Triangles that contain a 90-degree angle, called *right triangles*, have sides and angles that display particular relationships. These relationships have been exploited for centuries in such fields as surveying, building, and engineering; their study is called *trigonometry.*

This section is by no means a complete introduction to trigonometry, but the fundamental trigonometric functions *sine*, *cosine*, and *tangent* are shown in figure 1.7. For any right triangle *ABC* of any size and with right angle *C*, the illustrated ratios hold. These ratios have been computed and formalized over the years so that they are available now in tables for reference.

In Logo, these basic trigonometric ratios are available as the primitives **SIN**, **COS**, and **TAN**. They all need to be given an angle measurement, in degrees, as input. They output the appropriate ratio for that angle and function.

In Apple Logo, there is no **TAN**. If you are using Apple Logo or some other version that does not have **TAN**, you can define your own function for the tangent of an angle:

```
TO TAN :ANGLE
OUTPUT (SIN :ANGLE) / (COS :ANGLE)
END
```

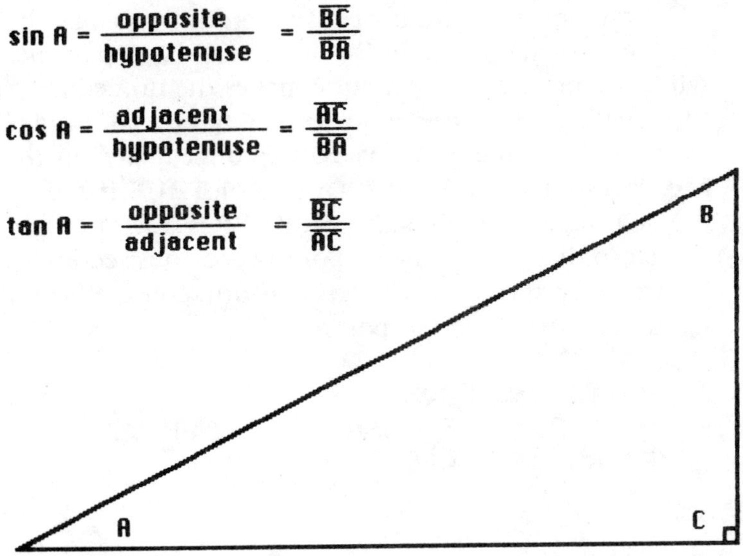

$$\sin A = \frac{\text{opposite}}{\text{hypotenuse}} = \frac{\overline{BC}}{\overline{BA}}$$

$$\cos A = \frac{\text{adjacent}}{\text{hypotenuse}} = \frac{\overline{AC}}{\overline{BA}}$$

$$\tan A = \frac{\text{opposite}}{\text{adjacent}} = \frac{\overline{BC}}{\overline{AC}}$$

Figure 1.7
Trigonometric functions

You can try out **SIN**, **COS**, and **TAN** with commands like these:

```
PRINT SIN 45
PRINT COS 197
PRINT TAN 36
```

To get an idea of the range of values of these functions, let's write a short test procedure to print the **SIN** of all angles from 0 to 360 degrees:

```
TO SINETEST :ANGLE
IF :ANGLE > 360 [STOP]
PRINT SENTENCE :ANGLE SIN :ANGLE
SINETEST :ANGLE + 1
END
```

You can run this now by typing **SINETEST 0**. You should see a growing column of numbers, representing the angle and the **SIN** of the angle, for angles from 0 to 360 degrees. The primitive **SENTENCE**, explained fully in chapter 3, is used in this procedure to combine the angle and its **SIN** into the printed output line.

Unfortunately, this procedure scrolls by so quickly that you may not be able to keep up with it. But we can add a step so that pressing any key while the procedure is running makes the procedure pause and wait for the user to press the <return> key before continuing. To do this, the procedure uses the primitive **KEYP** to see if any key on the keyboard has been pressed. **KEYP** gives a value of **TRUE** if the keyboard has been pressed and **FALSE** if it hasn't. If **KEYP** is true, then we can use a strategy similar to that used at the end of the previous section to wait for the user to press <return>. Let's define a procedure **WAIT.FOR.RETURN** to handle the details of the pause:

```
TO WAIT.FOR.RETURN
PRINT [PRESS <RETURN> TO GO ON...]
MAKE "GO.ON READLIST
END
```

With that tool at hand, we can now modify **SINETEST** so that the results do not scroll by uncontrollably:

```
TO SINETEST2 :ANGLE
IF KEYP [WAIT.FOR.RETURN]
IF :ANGLE > 360 [STOP]
PRINT SENTENCE :ANGLE SIN :ANGLE
SINETEST2 :ANGLE + 1
END
```

You can modify this procedure to see all the values for **COS** and **TAN**.

You might notice if you look at the values given by **SINETEST** that they are all less than 1 and that they change in a continuous manner. We can write a procedure to plot the value of an angle against its **SIN**. Because we are dealing with angles between 0 and 360 degrees, we need to transform the angle values to fit on the −100 to 100 coordinate grid.

There are two hundred spaces between −100 and 100, so if we make each space stand for 2 degrees, then we have room to spare. The first step, therefore, is to divide an angle in half to produce coordinates in the range 0 to 180. Next, we need to subtract 90 from this value to shift half the graph over into the left half of the screen. These calculations can be encapsulated in a Logo procedure:

```
TO SHOEHORN :ANGLE
OUTPUT (:ANGLE / 2) - 90
END
```

As a shoehorn might ease a foot into a too-small shoe, this procedure eases a value in the range 0 to 360 into the smaller −90 to 90 range. The converted angle values are used as the *x* coordinates in our graph.

Likewise, the values produced by **SIN** are not appropriate for graphing in raw form because they are all between 0 and 1. We need to multiply them all by a constant factor, say 50, to make them distinguishable when graphed. With these things in mind, we can define a procedure to graph a sine wave:

```
TO SINEWAVE :ANGLE
IF :ANGLE > 360 [STOP]
PENUP
SETPOS LIST SHOEHORN :ANGLE (SIN :ANGLE) * 50
PENDOWN
DOT POS    ; PUT DOT AT CURRENT POSITION
SINEWAVE :ANGLE + 1
END
```

This procedure uses two primitives not discussed before, **DOT** and **POS**. **POS** is the companion to **SETPOS**. **POS** gives the current turtle position rather than setting it. In this procedure, **SETPOS** is used to position the turtle according to the **:ANGLE** and **SIN** of the **:ANGLE**, and then **POS** is used to communicate the turtle's coordinates to the primitive **DOT**, which places a single dot at that location. This is a sequence that you use often when you are graphing coordinates in Logo: first **SETPOS**, then **DOT POS**. Try this out now by typing

```
CLEARSCREEN SINEWAVE 0
```

Figure 1.8 shows the results of **SINEWAVE**. This sort of continuously oscillating curve can be used to describe many natural phenomena, from ocean swells to sunlight. You can play around with the numbers used to fit the graph onto the grid. If you use a number other than 50 for multiplying the **SIN**, then you affect the amplitude of the curve. Dividing the angle by something other than 2 affects the frequency of the curve. If you divide by more than 2, you can let the angles get bigger than 360 degrees. Experiment and see what you can discover.

A Surveying Problem

Finally, on a practical note, we can investigate a surveying application for trigonometry. Imagine that a person wants to build a bridge across a

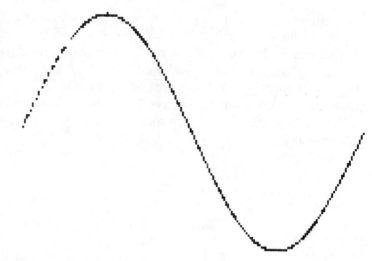

Figure 1.8
SINEWAVE 0

gorge but doesn't know how wide the gorge is (figure 1.9). The person calls in a surveyor. First the surveyor must set up a transit on one side of the gorge at point *A* and sight across to some object, say a tree, at point *B* on the other side. Then the surveyor must use the transit to sight along a right angle to some spot, point *C*, that is a known distance away from point *A*. For simplicity, we have chosen 100 feet for this example, but the known distance can be any value. Then the surveyor measures the angle at point *C* by sighting over to point *B*, finding that it is 49 degrees. At this point the surveyor can perform the calculations shown in figure 1.9.

The **TAN** of 49 degrees is equal to the length of the side opposite the 49-degree angle divided by the length of the side adjacent to the 49-degree angle. We don't know the length of the opposite side, but we know the length of the adjacent side, and we can find the **TAN** of 49 degrees. This information can be used to solve the equation for the unknown length of the opposite side.

If the surveyor has a portable computer in the field, he or she can write a short procedure to figure out the distance across the gorge on the basis of the initial observations:

```
TO DISTANCE.ACROSS :ANGLE :ADJACENT
OUTPUT (TAN :ANGLE) * :ADJACENT
END
```

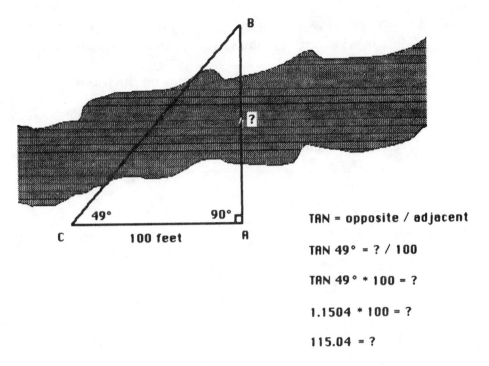

TAN = opposite / adjacent

TAN 49° = ? / 100

TAN 49° * 100 = ?

1.1504 * 100 = ?

115.04 = ?

Figure 1.9
Bridging a gorge

For the situation illustrated in figure 1.9, the surveyor types in

```
DISTANCE.ACROSS 49 100
```

and gets 115.04 as the distance across the gorge.

This example shows just one of the many ways trigonometry can be used in the everyday world.

SUMMARY ───────────────

This chapter has introduced several features of the Logo graphics world, including both turtle graphics and coordinate graphics. Logo graphics is too large a subect to cover in one chapter; indeed, whole books have been written on it. In particular, *Turtle Geometry* by Harold Abelson and Andrea diSessa (Appendix D) is an excellent and exhaustive resource.

The next chapter deals with recursion and turtle graphics. It shows more of what turtle graphics can do and also explains and lets you work with *recursion*.

The rest of the book concentrates on the list-processing aspects of Logo and uses turtle graphics only occasionally to illustrate a topic under discussion. In this way graphics is treated as part of a whole system rather than an end in itself. I think you will find the rest of the Logo system every bit as exciting and open-ended as you found turtle graphics.

2 RECURSIVE GRAPHICS

POLYSPI

Tail Recursion versus Internal Recursion

A Stack of Triangles

Using Levels to Control Recursion

Many Triangles

CORNERPOLY

SNOWFLAKE

Space-Filling Curves

Summary

In the previous chapter we talked about many different types of turtle graphics projects. Using the turtle is an excellent way to explore the world of geometry. Using the turtle is also a good way to learn about *recursion*. The examples in this chapter will allow you to watch both *tail recursion* and *internal recursion* at work. You will see how Logo can keep track of local input variables in many different copies of the same procedure as a string of recursive calls is played out. Once you master the concepts here, you will be ready to understand the recursive projects that come in the later chapters.

POLYSPI

POLYSPI is short for *polyspiral*, and it has become almost a cliché in the world of Logo programming. **POLYSPI** shows how recursion can be used to create a simple procedure that can produce a great variety of designs. In **POLYSPI**, the turtle moves forward and turns, over and over again. Each new move forward is longer than the one before, but the turn angle remains the same. Playing turtle with a pencil and paper, you can see that **POLYSPI** creates expanding spirals. Use the following procedure to create such spirals with the computer:

```
TO POLYSPI :LENGTH :ANGLE :CHANGE
FORWARD :LENGTH
RIGHT :ANGLE
POLYSPI (:LENGTH + :CHANGE) :ANGLE :CHANGE
END
```

When you use this procedure, you must provide three inputs: the length of the first side, the constant angle of turn, and the constant amount of change in length, as in

```
POLYSPI 5 91 5
```

The value of the **:LENGTH** input is changed by the recursive call in the last step. When **POLYSPI** is called at that point, the first input, which determines the amount of forward motion, will be changed to the sum of the value of the current **:LENGTH** plus the value of **:CHANGE**. This addition is cumulative: this new value of **:LENGTH** is used as the current value the next time through. To clarify this feature, we can write it out in the procedure like this:

```
TO POLYSPI2 :LENGTH :ANGLE :CHANGE
FORWARD :LENGTH
RIGHT :ANGLE
MAKE "LENGTH :LENGTH + :CHANGE
POLYSPI2 :LENGTH :ANGLE :CHANGE
END
```

This version first changes the value of **LENGTH** and then feeds the new value to the recursive call. The original version is desirable for its efficiency in taking care of changing the value of **LENGTH** and making the recursive call in the same step.

Note that neither of these procedures stops on its own. You must use <control> **G** to stop them. This points up a characteristic of all recursive procedures: they must have some sort of step that checks for a condition under which they must stop. In this case, you can have the procedure check the length of the forward motion each time and stop if it is greater than 100. The new procedure looks like this:

```
TO POLYSPI3 :LENGTH :ANGLE :CHANGE
IF :LENGTH > 100 [STOP]
FORWARD :LENGTH
RIGHT :ANGLE
POLYSPI3 (:LENGTH + :CHANGE) :ANGLE :CHANGE
END
```

Recursive procedures must know when to stop. There are many factors that you might want to use as stop checkpoints. Because **:LENGTH > 100** is not an appropriate condition for stopping when you use **POLYSPI3** with a negative value for **:CHANGE**, you may want to try different stopping conditions for **POLYSPI**, such as **:LENGTH < 5** (or either **XCOR** or **YCOR** such that the turtle is off the screen). Figures 2.1 through 2.3 show some examples of polyspiral drawings with various input values. Take some time to experiment with your own values. See if you can predict what your values will produce before you watch the turtle draw the polyspiral.

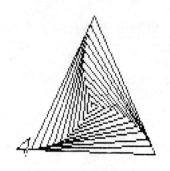

Figure 2.1
POLYSPI3 3 121 3

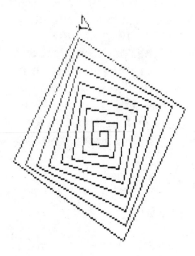

Figure 2.2
POLYSPI3 5 91 5

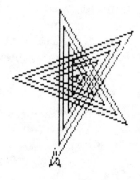

Figure 2.3
POLYSPI3 3 144 5

If you find a certain combination of inputs to **POLYSPI3** that you particularly like, you can define a separate procedure to call **POLYSPI3** with those inputs. For example, you can define the following procedure:

```
TO MY.FAVORITE
POLYSPI3 5 121 3
END
```

This allows you to identify your favorite designs with meaningful procedure names and frees you from remembering the numbers needed as inputs. You are building a friendly shell around the **POLYSPI3** procedure that makes it easier to use.

TAIL RECURSION VERSUS INTERNAL RECURSION

The recursive call in **POLYSPI** doesn't come until the last step in the procedure. The recursion that results is known as *tail recursion*. Looping structures available in other computer languages achieve a similar effect. Appendix A discusses how tail recursion is recognized by Logo to be simple looping. The next few projects in this chapter use *internal recursion*: the recursive call is not the last step in the procedure. This kind of recursion is somewhat more subtle than tail recursion. A procedure with an internal recursive call is interrupted in midstream and then must resume execution when the recursive call terminates. To allow this, Logo must keep track of the local input variables for all the recursive copies of the original procedure and also the return address of all the procedures that have been interrupted. This housekeeping is automatic, and the user does not have to worry about it but must keep in mind that it takes extra time and memory.

By watching the turtle demonstrate this type of recursion, you can gain an understanding of the subtleties of recursion in general. That understanding will be of use when you meet recursive procedures that involve words and lists, in later chapters.

A STACK OF TRIANGLES

Imagine the steps that the turtle has to execute in order to draw an equilateral triangle, starting at the midpoint of the base, as shown in figure 2.4. Allowing for an input so we can make the triangle any size, the

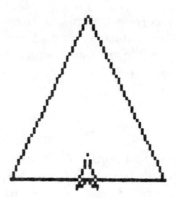

Figure 2.4
The turtle's rendering of an
equilateral triangle

procedure would look something like this next procedure. At each point at which the turtle reaches a corner of the triangle, there is a comment to mark the spot:

```
TO TRI :SIZE
LEFT 90
FORWARD :SIZE / 2
; FIRST CORNER
RIGHT 120
FORWARD :SIZE
; SECOND CORNER
RIGHT 120
FORWARD :SIZE
; THIRD CORNER
RIGHT 120
FORWARD :SIZE / 2
RIGHT 90   ; RETURN TO ORIGINAL HEADING
END
```

Now you can try this procedure with various inputs, such as **TRI 40** and **TRI 100**. Once you have seen that **TRI** draws a triangle of any size and returns the turtle to its original position and heading, imagine what the drawing would look like if at the second (top) corner (the apex) of the triangle the turtle drew a smaller version of the same triangle, as pictured in figure 2.5. Now you can see why the corners were marked in the original procedure.

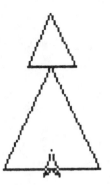

Figure 2.5
Stacked triangles

Figures 2.6 through 2.9 show how the turtle would have to look at several stages of drawing stacked triangles. Figure 2.6 shows the turtle just as it reaches the apex of the larger triangle. Figure 2.7 shows the result of the necessary left turn of 30 degrees to line up the turtle for the smaller triangle. Figure 2.8 shows the turtle after it has drawn the smaller triangle. Now note how the smaller-triangle procedure leaves the turtle in the position and heading in which the procedure found the turtle: figure 2.9 shows the turtle after a right turn of 30 degrees to restore its original heading, as in figure 2.6. At this point the original triangle procedure would continue drawing the rest of the big triangle.

From this you can see that we need some way to interrupt the main triangle procedure at the apex, turn the turtle left 30 degrees, draw a smaller triangle, turn the turtle right 30 degrees, and then return control to the main procedure. Since the smaller triangle can be drawn by the same procedure as the main triangle, recursion is the best way to accomplish this interruption.

Actually, viewing all procedure calls as interruptions of the main procedure is a good way of looking at Logo programming in general. When a procedure is going along, it takes its steps one at a time, executing each one and then going on to the next. Recursion works in just this way, except that the procedure makes a separate copy of itself, goes off to execute that copy, and then returns to finish its original version after the recursive copy is executed.

The difference between tail recursion and internal recursion is that tail recursion involves no leftover steps for the original version of the procedure to perform when execution of the recursive copy is finished, so the entire string of calls simply ends. After internal recursion, there are

Figure 2.6
The turtle as it reaches the
apex of the first triangle

Figure 2.7
The turtle after it turns left
30 degrees

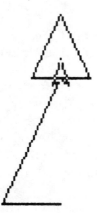

Figure 2.8
The turtle after it draws the
second triangle

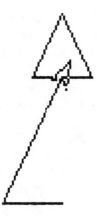

Figure 2.9
The turtle after it turns right
30 degrees

still steps to be performed in the original version of the procedure, so the system must do more housekeeping to keep track of all the copies. As a programmer, you can treat either kind of recursive call much as you treat any other procedure or primitive call, as long as there is some conditional check to make sure that the recursion doesn't spiral off infinitely.

Getting back to our triangle example, if we insert a recursive call to **TRI** at the second corner (marked by the comment), sandwiched between inserted left and right turns of 30 degrees, then we should be able to draw a complete triangle with a triangle at its apex. Of course, the smaller triangle at the apex is drawn by the same procedure as the main triangle, so it too has a triangle at its apex. And, of course, the smallest triangle at the apex of the smaller triangle will have an even smaller triangle at its apex, and. . . . We are back in the hall of mirrors again unless we add a step to **TRI** to tell it when to stop recursion. Let's stop when the **:SIZE** of the triangle is less than 10. Coupling this conditional with the turns and recursive calls inserted at the second corner, we get

```
TO TRISTACK :SIZE
IF :SIZE < 10 [STOP]
LEFT 90
FORWARD :SIZE / 2
; FIRST CORNER
RIGHT 120
FORWARD :SIZE
LEFT 30 TRISTACK :SIZE / 2 RIGHT 30    ; APEX
RIGHT 120
FORWARD :SIZE
; THIRD CORNER
RIGHT 120
FORWARD :SIZE / 2
RIGHT 90
END
```

The key to this procedure is the fact that each call to **TRISTACK** returns the turtle to the position and heading with which it started. This way, each level of recursion is transparent to the levels above and below it. When the turtle reaches the apex of a triangle, it doesn't really matter whether or not it draws a smaller triangle there. Either way, interrupted or not, the turtle is in the correct position to finish the rest of the triangle that it started.

The other property of Logo that makes this procedure work is that each recursive copy of **TRISTACK** keeps its own value of **:SIZE** separate from the other copies. Thus, when the topmost triangle is completed and control returns to the procedure for the next smallest triangle, that procedure remembers the **:SIZE** of that triangle, and so on back down to the original triangle.

The real advantage of recursion is that it allows you to write elegant procedures that operate on almost any level of complexity. If you call **TRISTACK 19**, then you get a single main triangle with no triangle at the top corner. **TRISTACK 60**, on the other hand, gives you a figure almost like a Christmas tree. Figures 2.10 and 2.11 show the results of two different calls to **TRISTACK**.

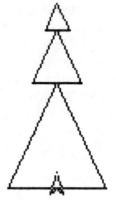

Figure 2.10
TRISTACK 19

Figure 2.11
TRISTACK 60

USING LEVELS TO CONTROL RECURSION ——————

The conditional step that we used in **TRISTACK** was to check the **:SIZE** of the triangles. Although this is one way to do it, there is a more direct way to control the amount of recursion that occurs. You can introduce another input variable into **TRISTACK**, called **:LEVEL**. **:LEVEL** tells the procedure how many times you want it to perform recursion. Using a **:LEVEL** of 1 gets you only the main triangle, using a **:LEVEL** of 2 gets you the main triangle with one triangle on its apex, and so on. Each recursive call decreases the **:LEVEL** by 1 and also cuts the **:SIZE** in half:

```
TO TRISTACK2 :SIZE :LEVEL
IF :LEVEL < 1 [STOP]
LEFT 90
FORWARD :SIZE / 2
; FIRST CORNER
RIGHT 120
FORWARD :SIZE
LEFT 30 TRISTACK2 :SIZE / 2 :LEVEL - 1 RIGHT 30
RIGHT 120
FORWARD :SIZE
; THIRD CORNER
RIGHT 120
FORWARD :SIZE / 2
RIGHT 90
END
```

The conditional step in this procedure checks to see if **:LEVEL** is less than 1. When the **:LEVEL** is 0, then no triangle is drawn.

Once you have this procedure entered, you can watch it operate by giving commands like

```
TRISTACK 100 1
TRISTACK 75 5
```

This is a good way to see how the interrupt model can help explain recursion. You can see that the procedure starts each level of triangle by drawing the first half of the figure, but may be interrupted by a recursive call at the top corner. At that point, the procedure for the smaller triangle takes over and the original procedure has to wait until the smaller triangle is done before it can complete its drawing. The smaller triangle may also be interrupted so that an even smaller triangle can be drawn at its apex. This train of interruption continues until the level has been reduced to 0, at which point the recursive interruptions stop and the routine for the smallest figure is allowed to complete its drawing, then the routine for the next largest, and so on until finally the original triangle is completed. The first one started is the last one finished.

In this situation Logo's slowness is probably beneficial, in that it allows you to visually follow the process of recursive control more easily.

MANY TRIANGLES —————————————————————————————

Now let's make a procedure to draw smaller triangles at all three corners instead of drawing a smaller copy of the triangle at the top corner only. This procedure is conceptually very similar to the one we just used, but while with just one triangle on the top corner of a main triangle the flow of control may not be too hard for you to follow, when the new triangle starts to have a triangle on each of its corners, then it may be harder to keep all the interrupted procedures in their correct order.

In this new procedure, the main triangle is interrupted three times before it is able to finish. The recursively called procedures at corners may themselves be interrupted before they can finish. Luckily, Logo is able to keep track of all this by keeping local copies of **:SIZE** and **:LEVEL** for each copy of the recursive procedure. You don't have to be concerned about these details as long as each interruption upon completion returns the turtle where it was, so that the interrupted procedure can proceed as if nothing had happened.

The procedure to draw a triangle with many triangles at each of its three corners is an adaptation of **TRISTACK2**:

```
TO MANYTRI :SIZE :LEVEL
IF :LEVEL < 1 [STOP]
LEFT 90
FORWARD :SIZE / 2
LEFT 30 MANYTRI :SIZE / 2 :LEVEL - 1 RIGHT 30
RIGHT 120
FORWARD :SIZE
LEFT 30 MANYTRI :SIZE / 2 :LEVEL - 1 RIGHT 30
RIGHT 120
FORWARD :SIZE
LEFT 30 MANYTRI :SIZE / 2 :LEVEL - 1 RIGHT 30
RIGHT 120
FORWARD :SIZE / 2
RIGHT 90
END
```

Figures 2.12 through 2.14 show **MANYTRI** on the first three levels. You can see that the corner triangles on the main triangle in the level 2 figure are actually level 1 figures, and that the corners of the main triangle in the level 3 drawing are adorned with level 2 figures. You will find that this kind of abstraction is helpful when you are designing your own recursive procedures.

Once you grasp the interrupt concept for recursion in a simple procedure like **TRISTACK**, then the leap to a more complex procedure like **MANYTRI** is not so difficult. Both procedures are driven by the same principles, after all.

CORNERPOLY

Applying the concepts of **MANYTRI** more generally, we can write a procedure that draws a polygon with an arbitrary number of sides, with smaller versions of the figure on each corner. In order to do this we need to add an input that tells the number of sides of the basic polygon. The total number of degrees, 360, is divided by the number of sides to determine the exterior angles that the turtle must turn to draw the main figure. Remember that it took three 120-degree turns to construct an equilateral triangle.

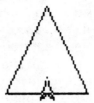

Figure 2.12
MANYTRI 50 1

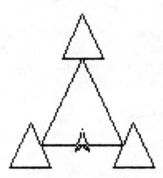

Figure 2.13
MANYTRI 50 2

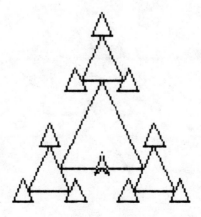

Figure 2.14
MANYTRI 50 3

The number of sides can also be used to figure out the angle that the turtle must turn to line up for the recursive polygons on each corner. Figure 2.15 shows that the exterior angle and the internal angle of the base polygon (in this case, a triangle) add up to 180 degrees. In order to line up the turtle for the corner polygons, we must turn it half as much as the interior angle so as to split the angle. In the case of the triangle, we turn the turtle 30 degrees to split the 60-degree interior angle before drawing the recursive triangles. This analysis translates into the following Logo statement:

```
LEFT (180 - (360 / :SIDES)) / 2
```

This statement takes the exterior angle, determined by **360 / :SIDES**, subtracts it from 180 to calculate the interior angle, and then divides by 2. This same calculation is done for the right turn that realigns the turtle after the recursion is finished:

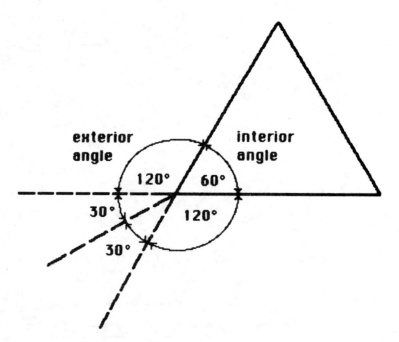

Figure 2.15
Figuring how much the
turtle must turn to draw
a recursive polygon

```
TO CORNERPOLY :SIDES :LENGTH :LEVEL
IF :LEVEL < 1 [STOP]
LEFT 90 FORWARD :LENGTH / 2
REPEAT :SIDES [LEFT (180 - (360 / :SIDES)) / 2
                CORNERPOLY :SIDES
                           :LENGTH / 2
                           :LEVEL - 1
                RIGHT (180 - (360 / :SIDES)) / 2
                RIGHT 360 / :SIDES
                FORWARD :LENGTH
                ]
BACK :LENGTH / 2
RIGHT 90
END
```

Because of the way the **REPEAT** statement draws the sides of the polygon, we must insert an additional step to move the turtle back to the midpoint of the base line.

This procedure gives you a lot of flexibility in choosing the kind of figure that you want. The first input tells how many sides the base figure has. The second input is the length of each line in the level 1 polygon. The third input tells how many levels the procedure recursively executes. A level 1 procedure draws only the base figure, with no polygons on its corners. A level 2 procedure draws the base polygon with smaller level 1 polygons on all its corners. Level 3 draws the base figure with smaller level 2 figures on the corners. Figures 2.16 through 2.19 show some different figures that can be drawn with **CORNERPOLY**.

Experiment with your own inputs to come up with your favorite designs. As we did earlier with **POLYSPI3**, you can take your favorite **CORNERPOLY** and put it into a convenient shell procedure to save you the trouble of remembering which combination of inputs gives a pleasing result. If you really like the design drawn by **CORNERPOLY 6 50 4**, for instance, then you can define the following procedure:

```
TO BEAUTY
CORNERPOLY 6 50 4
END
```

When you do this sort of thing, you exploit Logo's procedural ability to create your own personal programming language. You can use this ability to package powerful data-manipulation tools into procedures, or simply to remember how to draw pretty pictures for yourself and others.

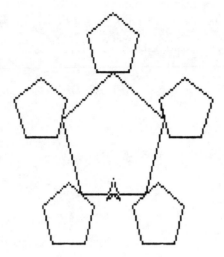

Figure 2.16
CORNERPOLY 5 40 2

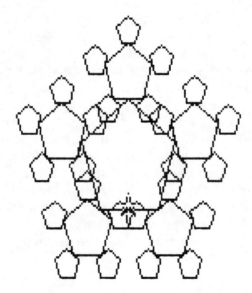

Figure 2.17
CORNERPOLY 5 35 3

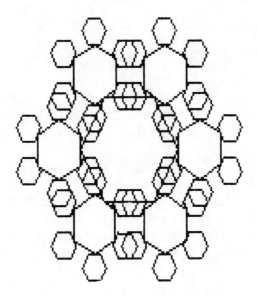

Figure 2.18
CORNERPOLY 6 30 3

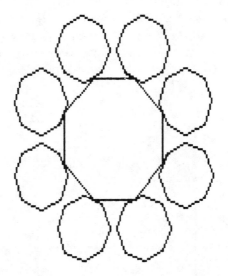

Figure 2.19
CORNERPOLY 8 25 2

SNOWFLAKE

For this next project, imagine that you want the turtle to go from one point to another. Obviously, the simplest way to get it to do that would be to have it draw a straight line connecting the two points, as shown in figure 2.20. Now imagine that instead of having the turtle go straight from one point to the other you get it to make a detour on the way, as shown in figure 2.21.

The path shown in figure 2.21 consists of four straight line segments. Now—and here comes the recursive part—imagine that instead of letting the turtle draw these four straight line segments you make the turtle take the same sort of detour four times (figure 2.22).

The relationship between the straight line in figure 2.20 and the four line segments in figure 2.21 is the same as the relationship between each of the lines in figure 2.21 and the corresponding sections of figure 2.22. Of course, this relationship can be extended to yet another level by taking the many straight line segments in figure 2.22 and making them take detours also.

Once you see this recursive relationship, then you can express that relationship in Logo. The procedure that we make needs two inputs, **:LENGTH** and **:LEVEL**. The **:LENGTH** input is needed because each time a line segment is broken into smaller line segments, they must be shorter, and because, since we are going to use the same procedure to draw all the segments, the procedure must be able to draw them any length. The

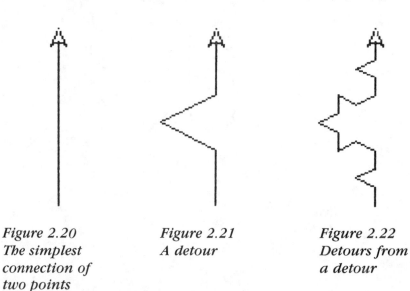

Figure 2.20
The simplest
connection of
two points

Figure 2.21
A detour

Figure 2.22
Detours from
a detour

:LEVEL input is used to tell the procedure how deeply to perform recursion. We could instead use some sort of check on how **:LENGTH** is being reduced and stop when it gets too small, but the concept of levels is more directly related to the depth of recursion.

The turns that guide the detour are a **LEFT 60**, a **RIGHT 120**, and another **LEFT 60**. The total net turn is 0 degrees, so the turtle ends up headed in the direction in which it started. Each of the legs that connect these turns is the same length.

Looking back at figures 2.20 through 2.22, you can see that figure 2.20 represents a level 0 procedure, figure 2.21 a level 1 procedure, and figure 2.22 a level 2 procedure. To draw a level 0 figure, the procedure must simply move the turtle forward the input length, and stop. To draw a level 1 figure, the procedure must get the turtle to take the following steps (keep in mind that a level 0 figure is just a straight line):

draw a smaller (one-third size) level 0 figure
turn left 60 degrees
draw a smaller (one-third size) level 0 figure
turn right 120 degrees
draw a smaller (one-third size) level 0 figure
turn left 60 degres
draw a smaller (one-third size) level 0 figure

Carrying this one step further, you can see that to draw a level 2 figure, as shown in figure 2.22, the procedure would have to get the turtle to perform the steps outlined above but drawing level 1 figures instead of level 0 figures at each turn. Of course, the procedure to draw level 1 figures would have to go ahead and draw the level 0 lines, but you don't have to think about that at this point. It is enough for you to know that a level 2 figure is made up simply of four level 1 figures tied together with turns.

This is a very important concept because understanding it frees you from the necessity of thinking more than one level away from where you are at any time. Once you know what a level 0 figure looks like, then you can use it to construct level 1 figures. And once you can make level 1 figures, you can use them to make level 2 figures, and so on through the higher levels. A level 6 figure is made by following the steps that were outlined above, drawing four level 5 figures connected by turns. Generalizing from this, a level n figure is made up of four level $(n - 1)$ figures. With these abstractions in mind, you can see that the procedure follows from the outlined steps:

```
TO SEGMENT :LENGTH :LEVEL
IF :LEVEL < 1 [FORWARD :LENGTH STOP]
SEGMENT :LENGTH / 3 :LEVEL - 1
LEFT 60
SEGMENT :LENGTH / 3 :LEVEL - 1
RIGHT 120
SEGMENT :LENGTH / 3 :LEVEL - 1
LEFT 60
SEGMENT :LENGTH / 3 :LEVEL - 1
END
```

You can try this procedure with commands such as

```
SEGMENT 100 0
SEGMENT 100 1
SEGMENT 100 5
```

Next you can join three **SEGMENT**s into a closed curve. At level 0, this closed curve is an equilateral triangle. At higher levels it can resemble a snowflake:

```
TO SNOWFLAKE :SIZE :LEVEL
REPEAT 3 [SEGMENT :SIZE :LEVEL RIGHT 120]
END
```

Figures 2.23 through 2.25 show the first three levels of **SNOWFLAKE**.

It is not necessary that **SNOWFLAKE** be composed of just three **SEGMENT**s. It is easy to imagine **SNOWFLAKE**s made up of four, five, or ten **SEGMENT**s linked together with the proper turns. The procedure to create such **SNOWFLAKE**s needs another input to tell how many sides the **SNOWFLAKE** has. It can look like this:

```
TO SNOWFLAKE2 :SIZE :LEVEL :NUM.SIDES
REPEAT :NUM.SIDES [SEGMENT :SIZE :LEVEL
                   RIGHT 360 / :NUM.SIDES
                   ]
END
```

The **:NUM.SIDES** input is used to determine the number of repetitions and also the number of degrees of turn needed at each corner. This is a good example of how you can make an interesting Logo procedure

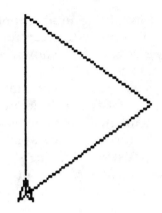

Figure 2.23
SNOWFLAKE 80 0

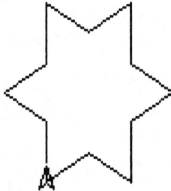

Figure 2.24
SNOWFLAKE 80 1

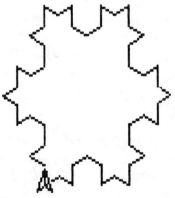

Figure 2.25
SNOWFLAKE 80 2

more versatile by adding another input. With very little additional effort on your part, this procedure can now produce a wide variety of drawings. Figures 2.26 and 2.27 show, for instance, **SNOWFLAKE2 50 2 6** and **SNOWFLAKE2 50 2 4**.

You might also want to experiment with changing the path taken by **SEGMENT**. Remember that in its original form the detour consisted of four line segments that form the pattern shown in figure 2.21. Imagine instead that the turtle follows a path as shown in figure 2.28 (page 48). This detour consists of five line segments, all of the same length, connected by turns. The structure of the procedure to draw this shape is similar in concept to the original **SEGMENT**:

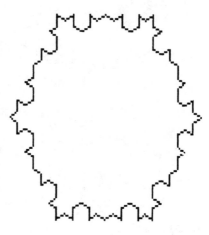

Figure 2.26
SNOWFLAKE2 50 2 6

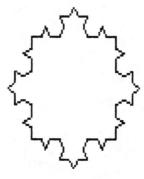

Figure 2.27
SNOWFLAKE2 50 2 4

```
TO NEWSEGMENT :LENGTH :LEVEL
IF :LEVEL < 1 [FORWARD :LENGTH STOP]
NEWSEGMENT :LENGTH / 2 :LEVEL - 1
LEFT 120
NEWSEGMENT :LENGTH / 2 :LEVEL - 1
RIGHT 120
NEWSEGMENT :LENGTH / 2 :LEVEL - 1
RIGHT 120
NEWSEGMENT :LENGTH / 2 :LEVEL - 1
LEFT 120
NEWSEGMENT :LENGTH / 2 :LEVEL - 1
END
```

Figure 2.28 is a level 1 drawing by **NEWSEGMENT**. Of course, just as with **SEGMENT**, a level 0 drawing is simply a straight line. At the higher levels **NEWSEGMENT** is interesting because it begins to overlap itself. Figures 2.29 and 2.30 show a level 2 drawing and a level 3 drawing by **NEWSEGMENT**.

You might want to explore other types of **SEGMENT**s that overlap themselves. Consider the drawing in figure 2.31 (page 49). The details of the procedure are left to you, but the structure is very similar to that of **SEGMENT** and **NEWSEGMENT**. Just remember to keep all the line segments the same length.

As you may have guessed, you can use any of these variant segment procedures in **SNOWFLAKE** or **SNOWFLAKE2** simply by substituting them in place of **SEGMENT**. Again, notice Logo's strength as a modular programming language. Logo's ability to accept variant forms within an overall structure gives you great creative power and flexibility. Once you understand the fundamental concepts that govern these recursive segments, you should be able to create many different forms and apply them to produce drawings as varied as real snowflakes.

SPACE-FILLING CURVES —————————————————————————

Imagine that the turtle sits on the bottom corner of a square diamond (figure 2.32, page 50) and you want to get it to the opposite corner. Of course, the easiest way is to have the turtle draw a straight line equal to the diagonal of the square, shown by the dotted line in figure 2.32. Once the turtle has done this, we can say the turtle has *traversed* the square.

Now imagine that the square is divided into nine smaller squares, all equal in size. As you can see in figure 2.33 (page 51), the turtle can

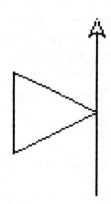

Figure 2.28
Another detour

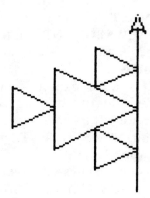

Figure 2.29
NEWSEGMENT, level 2

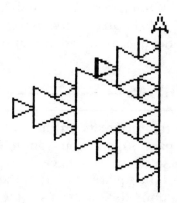

Figure 2.30
NEWSEGMENT, level 3

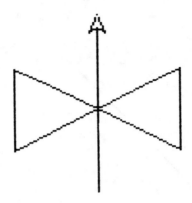

Figure 2.31
A drawing produced by a procedure similar in
structure to SEGMENT and NEWSEGMENT

traverse each of these squares in the same way as it traversed the original big square. The corners of the smaller squares are connected in such a way that the turtle can move from one to the next, as shown by the numbers and dotted pathway in figure 2.33.

At each new corner, the turtle must make a turn to align itself with the new diagonal, but it can use the same technique to actually traverse each of the smaller squares. For a moment, let's ignore the details of the procedure that traverses each square and concentrate on the turns that the turtle must make to align itself with the diagonals of the nine smaller squares. If it follows the path shown in figure 2.33, then the turtle is carrying out a set of instructions that is something like this:

traverse square 1
left 90
traverse square 2
right 90
traverse square 3
right 90
traverse square 4
right 90
traverse square 5
left 90
traverse square 6
left 90
traverse square 7
left 90

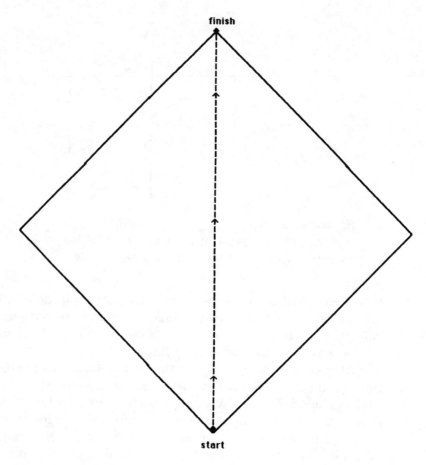

Figure 2.32
Traversing a square

traverse square 8
right 90
traverse square 9

When we translate this into a Logo procedure, we can combine some of the consecutive right turns and left turns into **REPEAT** statements, but for now just follow the steps listed above and make sure that you can see how the turtle winds its way through the squares.

Exploring recursion, we can take each of the nine squares and divide it into nine even smaller squares. In the same way as figure 2.33 is made up of nine miniature figure 2.32s connected by turns, a figure can be

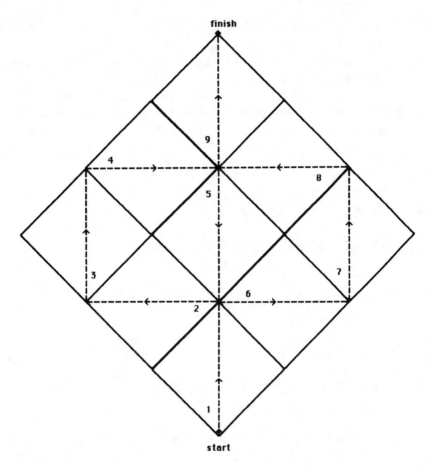

Figure 2.33
Traversing nine square

made up of nine smaller figure 2.33s. In both figure 2.32 and figure 2.33 the turtle starts at the lower corner and ends up at the opposite corner of the square. This means that either figure may be drawn with the set of turns outlined above with no modification.

Translating all this into a Logo procedure, we must use two inputs: **:SIZE** and **:LEVEL**. We need **:SIZE** since the procedure is called upon to draw paths through squares of many different sizes. The **:LEVEL** input is used in the same way as in other procedures in this chapter to determine the amount of recursion that takes place. A level 0 procedure draws a path like the dotted line in figure 2.32, and a level 1 draws the dotted path in figure 2.33. The drawing that we imagined being made up of nine figure 2.33s can be drawn by a level 2 procedure.

Here you can see the same type of abstraction as you saw with the **SNOWFLAKE**s in the last section. A figure of any particular level is made up of figures of the next lowest level. This fact simplifies the code for our procedure because it means we need to think only one level away at any time. Going back and using the outline of turns as a guide, we can write the following procedure:

```
TO TRAVERSE :SIZE :LEVEL
IF :LEVEL = 0 [FORWARD :SIZE STOP]
TRAVERSE :SIZE / 3 :LEVEL - 1
LEFT 90
REPEAT 3 [TRAVERSE :SIZE / 3 :LEVEL - 1
          RIGHT 90
          ]
REPEAT 3 [TRAVERSE :SIZE / 3 :LEVEL - 1
          LEFT 90
          ]
TRAVERSE :SIZE / 3 :LEVEL - 1
RIGHT 90
TRAVERSE :SIZE / 3 :LEVEL - 1
END
```

The key to this procedure's recursive simplicity is the fact that a level 1 figure is made up of nine level 0 figures, and, furthermore, a level 2 figure is made up of nine level 1 figures. As a programmer, you have to know how to make only level 0 and 1 figures to open the possibility of much more complex figures through the power of recursion. Figures 2.34 through 2.36 show the first three levels (0, 1, and 2) of **TRAVERSE**. As you can see, **TRAVERSE** does not draw the outline of the squares. It just traces the path of the turtle as it travels through the imaginary recursively divided space.

As it is written right now, **TRAVERSE** simply draws a straight line when it finally does cross one of the level 0 squares. Imagine that instead of going from one point to the other in a straight line, the turtle takes a detour like the one we developed for the procedure **SEGMENT** in the last section on **SNOWFLAKE**s. Let's use a level 1 **SEGMENT** in place of the

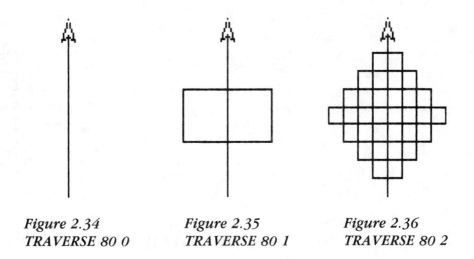

Figure 2.34
TRAVERSE 80 0

Figure 2.35
TRAVERSE 80 1

Figure 2.36
TRAVERSE 80 2

straight line that crosses a level 0 square in **TRAVERSE**. To do that, we replace the step in **TRAVERSE**

```
IF :LEVEL = 0 [FORWARD :SIZE STOP]
```

with the step

```
IF :LEVEL = 0 [SEGMENT :SIZE 1 STOP]
```

(If you haven't defined **SEGMENT** yet, go back to the previous section of this chapter and type it in.) Figures 2.37 through 2.39 show three drawings made by this modified **TRAVERSE** procedure. The drawings have a figure-ground ambiguity that makes them reminiscent of the drawings of M. C. Escher. This is fitting because much of Escher's work was concerned with visual recursion.

You should try some of the other types of segments that were suggested in the **SNOWFLAKE** section as alternatives to the simple straight line in **TRAVERSE**. Using **NEWSEGMENT** instead of **SEGMENT** leads to some very interesting drawings with a modified **TRAVERSE**.

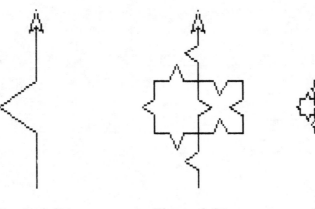

Figure 2.37
TRAVERSE2 80 0

Figure 2.38
TRAVERSE2 80 1

Figure 2.39
TRAVERSE2 80 2

SUMMARY

In this chapter we have used recursion to combine simple steps and turns into drawings that range from simple to very complex. We used both tail recursion, which involves a recursive call as the last step of the procedure and which imitates simple looping, and internal recursion, which involves recursive calls as steps other than the last step and which leads to more subtle effects.

Recursion can be understood as an interruption to the flow of a procedure. A recursive call effectively makes a separate copy of a procedure, a copy with its own local inputs. The original version of the procedure keeps its original inputs separate from the recursive copy so that they will be intact when the interruption ends and processing resumes on the original procedure. In this way, recursion is not so different from other procedure calls in Logo. The recursively called procedure can be viewed as just like any other procedure that, when called, interrupts the execution of the calling procedure, does its job, and then returns control to the original caller.

The procedures in this chapter illustrate the recursive process. They show the ability of recursive definitions to operate at any level of complexity from the mundane to the baroque.

Understanding the notion of *level*, which was introduced in this chapter to control the amount of recursion, is crucial to understanding how to write your own recursive routines. Once you grasp the fundamental concepts of recursion, you never have to think about more than one or two levels of a recursive solution at a time. The logical basis of recursive procedures is so strong that the programmer is freed to think abstractly about a problem and let Logo worry about the details of following the train of recursive execution back to its source. Thus, in a procedure like **SEGMENT** it is sufficient to say that at each turn the turtle should draw a **SEGMENT** of the next lowest level, and that definition will be good no matter what level you are trying to draw.

The *level* concept is important because it also controls when the recursion should stop. The ability to stop of recursive procedures is vital to their usefulness. In both the **SNOWFLAKE** and the space-filling procedures, the turtle doesn't actually draw a line until the procedure has worked its way down to level 0. The level 0s are then combined into level 1s, level 1s are combined into level 2s, and so on, up to an arbitrary predetermined level.

You will probably find that the resolution of the graphics available on your microcomputer limits the depth of recursion that is useful with these procedures, but you should be aware that with higher resolution these procedures can produce very complex figures. In later chapters we shall be using some of these same concepts of recursion to operate on words and numbers. Then the depth of recursion will not be limited by graphics resolution, and the benefits of arbitrarily deep recursion will become more apparent. Chapters 4, 6, and 7 make particularly heavy use of recursion for both graphic and nongraphic purposes. If you understand the concepts presented here, you are ready to tackle the projects in those chapters.

3 WORDS, LISTS, AND NUMBERS

Logo is probably best known for its turtle graphics. One of the goals of the original designers of Logo was to put together a language that would allow the user with a minimum amount of programming knowledge to easily create very interesting graphics. Turtle graphics certainly illustrates the designers' success in reaching this goal.

Turtle graphics is a hook to get people interested in controlling the computer. Logo, however, involves much more than turtle graphics. Logo has a powerful assortment of commands to manipulate both text and numbers.

This chapter will introduce most of the concepts fundamental to the use of these Logo commands. Much as a few simple turtle graphics commands can be combined to make complex designs, so a very few commands can be combined to produce powerful procedures to manipulate both words and numbers.

WORDS ─────────────────────────────

The basic unit of data in Logo is the *word*. A word is a string of characters that ends with a space. In some computer languages, especially BASIC, spaces are not important and can often be ignored. In many other programming languages you must use commas to separate words. Commas are not used in Logo. Rather, spaces are used to mark the end of one word and the beginning of another. A Logo word can be made up of letters, digits, or other printable characters. Thus a word can look like any of the following:

```
"FOO
"TRANSYLVANIA
"BOZO#1
"MY.PICTURE
123
"
```

Using a period to combine two words into one, as in **MY.PICTURE** (usually pronounced *my-dot-picture*), is an informal Logo convention.

The last two examples show two special cases of Logo words. A number is considered a Logo word even when it is not preceded by quotation marks. The last example, ", is a pair of quotation marks followed by a space. This is called the *empty word*.

As discussed in Appendix A, to get Logo to recognize a word as a literal string, you must precede it with quotation marks, as in **"FOO**. The quotation marks are a prefix operator, much like **FORWARD** or **RIGHT**. Just as **FORWARD** and **RIGHT** are primitives that take inputs and perform some action, so the quotation marks are a Logo primitive that takes a word as input, in this case **FOO**, and outputs the literal string of characters that make up that word. This is why there are no quotation marks in Logo at the end of a literal word, as is common in other computer languages. As discussed in Appendix A, words that do not have leading quotation marks are assumed by Logo to be names of procedures or primitives. Appendix A also discusses the way that Logo words can be interpreted as variables with associated values.

If you want to print a word on the screen, you use the Logo primitive **PRINT** or **TYPE**. The commands look like this:

```
PRINT "FOOTBALL
TYPE "BASKETBALL
```

The difference between **PRINT** and **TYPE** is that **PRINT** puts in a <return> after it is done, but **TYPE** leaves the cursor on the same line as the word. **TYPE** can be used when you want to put several words on the same line, as in

```
TYPE "THIS
TYPE "IS
TYPE "FUN
```

A more commonly used method for printing more than one word on a line is to put the words into a list. Using a list, you can rewrite the previous example as

```
PRINT [THIS IS FUN]
```

LISTS ─────────────────────────────────

Lists are the other main Logo data type. Lists are made up of words, other lists, or both. Lists can look like any of the following:

```
[APPLES]
[ORANGES PEACHES]
[GRAPES BANANAS [ORANGES LEMONS]]
[APPLES [MCINTOSH [GRANNY SMITH] PIPPIN]]
[]
```

The last example is the special case called the *empty list*. It is analogous to the empty word discussed in the previous section.

Notice that words inside list brackets do not need leading quotation marks. When Logo encounters a list, it does not go inside the outer brackets to evaluate any of the contents but rather treats the entire list as a single entity. Lists within lists are also treated as units. Thus, the first list shown below has four members, and the second list has two members, the second of which is itself a list. Lists within lists are often referred to as *sublists*:

```
[ONE TWO THREE FOUR]
[ONE [TWO THREE FOUR]]
```

Because a list can have another list as a member, we say that lists are *recursively defined*. Recursive procedures are often used to manipulate the data enclosed in lists. Understanding this connection between the structure of the data and the structure of the procedure that operates on the data is fundamental to thoughtful programming.

The next two sections of this chapter will be concerned with the Logo primitives that build lists and words and also take them apart. There are just a few fundamental commands to do these things, but you will find that they are flexible enough to allow sophisticated manipulation of words, lists, and numbers.

PUTTING THINGS TOGETHER ────────────────

The most basic command for combining in Logo is **WORD**. It is used to put two words together into one word. Here are some examples:

command	*result*
WORD "BASE "BALL	"BASEBALL
WORD "ROCKET 69	"ROCKET69
WORD "ITEM ".MINE	"ITEM.MINE
(WORD "FOO)	"FOO
(WORD "ONE "TWO "THREE)	"ONETWOTHREE

You can see from the examples that **WORD** usually takes two inputs, both of which must be either a word or a number. If you use **WORD** with more or less than two inputs, then the whole expression must be surrounded by parentheses, as shown in the last two examples. In many other computer languages, the parentheses are put around the inputs but not around the command. In Logo the parentheses are used to group both the command and the inputs.

Because **WORD** is a primitive that outputs its result, it can be used as input to other primitives and procedures. Indeed, in Apple Logo, if you type in

```
WORD "BROOM "STICK
```

all by itself, Logo responds with an error message:

```
I DON'T KNOW WHAT TO DO WITH BROOMSTICK
```

because it wants you to feed the output of **WORD** to some other primitive or procedure that will do something with it. One solution to this is to use **WORD** with the primitive **PRINT**:

```
PRINT WORD "BROOM "STICK
```

Other versions of Logo may be more forgiving than Apple Logo in this kind of situation. Dr. Logo, in the absence of any other command, will respond by just printing **BROOMSTICK** even if there is no explicit **PRINT** statement. Although the examples in this book are written in Dr. Logo, they generally adhere to the tighter Apple Logo restrictions for handling output from primitives and procedures. When you want something printed, it is best to specifically call the **PRINT** or **TYPE** command.

WORD can also be nested so that the output from one call is fed as input to another call to **WORD**:

```
PRINT WORD "UN WORD "COMMON "LY
```

This can also be expressed as

```
PRINT (WORD "UN "COMMON "LY)
```

As you might expect, **WORD** can be used only with words as input. It cannot be used to combine elements into lists. The next four primitives discussed are used to put lists together.

The first primitive you can use to put a list together is **LIST**. It takes two inputs, which may be words or numbers or lists, and outputs a list containing both inputs. Here are some examples:

command	*result*
`LIST "THE "CAT`	`[THE CAT]`
`LIST "THE [LONG ROAD]`	`[THE [LONG ROAD]]`
`LIST [THE] [LONG ROAD]`	`[[THE] [LONG ROAD]]`
`(LIST [A] "B [C])`	`[[A] B [C]]`
`(LIST [BIRD])`	`[[BIRD]]`

If you are using more or less than two inputs, you need to enclose the expression in parentheses, as shown by the last two examples. Also notice that **LIST** maintains the integrity of the items that you give it as input. If you give it two lists, they are combined into a single list with two members, both of which are lists.

The next primitive that you can use to combine things into lists is **SENTENCE**. Unlike **LIST**, **SENTENCE** does not necessarily put its inputs into a list unchanged. The output from **SENTENCE** is in some cases the same as it would be from **LIST**, but most of the time it is different. Compare these examples with the examples for **LIST**:

command	*result*
`SENTENCE "THE "CAT`	`[THE CAT]`
`SENTENCE "THE [LONG ROAD]`	`[THE LONG ROAD]`
`SENTENCE [THE] [LONG ROAD]`	`[THE LONG ROAD]`
`(SENTENCE [A] "B [C])`	`[A B C]`
`(SENTENCE [BIRD])`	`[BIRD]`

You can see that **SENTENCE** tends to produce lists with less internal structure: **SENTENCE** strips away outer brackets from its inputs before putting them into the output list. **SENTENCE** is often used to create lists that are to be printed. **LIST** is more often used to build lists with an internal structure that must be maintained, as when the sublists refer to some abstract data structure (see chapters 6 and 7, particularly). Notice also that **SENTENCE** can be used with more or less than two inputs if parentheses are used.

There are two more primitives that you can use to combine elements into lists. **FPUT** and **LPUT** stand for *first put* and *last put*, respectively. They always take two inputs and put the first input into the second input. Here are some examples:

command	*result*
FPUT "THE [LONG ROAD]	[THE LONG ROAD]
LPUT "THE [LONG ROAD]	[LONG ROAD THE]
FPUT [THE] [LONG ROAD]	[[THE] LONG ROAD]
LPUT [THE] [LONG ROAD]	[LONG ROAD [THE]]

Unlike the inputs to **LIST** and **SENTENCE**, which may be words or lists, the inputs to **FPUT** and **LPUT** are more restricted. The first input may be a word or a list. The second input, which is the destination for the first, must be a list. Thus, it is not correct to say **FPUT "FOO "BAR**. Also, you may not use **FPUT** or **LPUT** with more or less than two inputs.

FPUT and **LPUT** insert the first input as a member of the second input. If the first input is a list, then it is inserted as a list. If it is a word, then it is inserted as a word. You will find that **FPUT** is faster than **LPUT**, especially when the target list is very long.

The various actions of these four primitives are best shown by example. Figure 3.1 shows the results when these four primitives are applied to several sets of inputs. Experience will help you decide which primitive is most appropriate in various situations. In general, use **LIST**

LIST "ONE "TWO	[ONE TWO]
SENTENCE "ONE "TWO	[ONE TWO]
FPUT "ONE "TWO	----------
LPUT "ONE "TWO	----------
LIST "ONE [TWO]	[ONE [TWO]]
SENTENCE "ONE [TWO]	[ONE TWO]
FPUT "ONE [TWO]	[ONE TWO]
LPUT "ONE [TWO]	[TWO ONE]
LIST [ONE] [TWO]	[[ONE] [TWO]]
SENTENCE [ONE] [TWO]	[ONE TWO]
FPUT [ONE] [TWO]	[[ONE] TWO]
LPUT [ONE] [TWO]	[TWO [ONE]]
LIST [ONE] [[TWO] THREE]	[[ONE] [[TWO] THREE]]
SENTENCE [ONE] [[TWO] THREE]	[ONE [TWO] THREE]
FPUT [ONE] [[TWO] THREE]	[[ONE] [TWO] THREE]
LPUT [ONE] [[TWO] THREE]	[[TWO] THREE [ONE]]

Figure 3.1
Results of LIST, SENTENCE, FPUT, and LPUT

when it is important to maintain the sublist structure, as when the lists are used to store structured data. Use **SENTENCE** when the internal structure of the output list is not important, or even when you want to homogenize a list, as when you are preparing printed output. Finally, use **FPUT** and **LPUT** when you are adding elements to lists but don't want to disturb the internal structure of the sublists, as when you are updating a data list. Experiment with these four primitives.

TAKING THINGS APART ———————————————

Once you can put words and lists together, as shown in the previous section, then you want to be able also to take them apart. The primitives that do this operate on both words and lists with equal facility. With just four commands you can get at any part of a word or list.

Consider the list **[A B [C D] E]**. It has four members: **A**, **B**, **[C D]**, and **E**. One of the members is itself a list, but it is considered a unit within the larger list. There are four primitives that you can use to select part of this list: **FIRST**, **LAST**, **BUTFIRST**, and **BUTLAST**. Their actions are summarized below:

```
FIRST       selects the first element of its input
LAST        selects the last element of its input
BUTFIRST    selects all but the first element of its input
BUTLAST     selects all but the last element of its input
```

Note these examples:

command	*result*
FIRST [A B [C D] E]	A
LAST [A B [C D] E]	E
BUTFIRST [A B [C D] E]	[B [C D] E]
BUTLAST [A B [C D] E]	[A B [C D]]

At first glance, you might think, So what? The real power of these commands comes when they are combined, however. For instance, to get at the second element of a list, you can say

```
FIRST BUTFIRST [A B [C D] E]
```

which takes the **FIRST** of the **BUTFIRST** of the list. Logo expressions often seem to be evaluated from right to left. In the example above, the output of **BUTFIRST [A B [C D] E]**, which is **[B [C D] E]**, is given as input to **FIRST**, which then outputs **B**. These commands can be combined many levels deep to get at any element of a list.

You can also use these primitives to step through a list one member at a time, doing the same thing to each item. You generally do this by writing a recursive procedure with the list as an input. Each time the procedure executes, the first element of the list is operated upon; then the procedure is called recursively with the **BUTFIRST** of the list. This process proceeds until all members of the list have had the chance to be the first member. (We shall use this strategy extensively throughout the projects in the second half of this book.) For example, suppose you want to go through a list and print each member on a separate line. The arrangement might be called *pretty printing*. You can define a short procedure to do it:

```
TO PRETTYPRINT :LIST
IF EMPTYP :LIST [STOP]
PRINT FIRST :LIST
PRETTYPRINT BUTFIRST :LIST
END
```

Try this out with a few examples:

```
PRETTYPRINT [A B [C D] E]
PRETTYPRINT [ONE TWO THREE FOUR FIVE]
PRETTYPRINT "ALPHABET
```

The last example illustrates the fact that these commands work on words as well as lists. **FIRST** selects the first letter of a word, **LAST** selects the last letter, **BUTFIRST** selects all but the first letter, and **BUTLAST** selects all but the last letter.

PRETTYPRINT uses the primitive **EMPTYP** to see if the input list or word is empty, a condition signaling that all the members have been printed. You could have used

```
IF :LIST = [] [STOP]
```

instead of **IF EMPTYP :LIST [STOP]**, but that would limit this procedure's use to lists only. The nice thing about **EMPTYP** is that it will work for either an empty list or an empty word.

USING LISTS ——————————————————————

Although the word is the fundamental data structure in Logo, the list is more often used to guide programming strategy. Because the list is defined recursively (that is, it is made up of members that may also be lists), very often the procedures that are written to operate on lists are also recursive. The structure of your data virtually dictates the program structure you should use. Although it is possible to write programs in Logo that use the **GOTO** type of control common to nonstructured programming languages, this book will not do so.

Some of the recursive solutions developed in later chapters might run a little slower than nonrecursive ones, but we are interested in elegance. If you want speed, perhaps you should learn assembly language.

Lists can be used much as arrays are used in other computer languages. At its simplest, a list is just an ordered sequence of data objects, be they words or sublists. Just like an array, a list of this sort can be stepped through, one member at a time, until all its members have been encountered, as shown in the previous section with **PRETTYPRINT**. When a list is a simple sequence of items, then tail recursion is used to step through the list. Most Logo systems are able to treat tail recursion as simple looping, avoiding the high system overhead usually associated with recursion. (See Appendix A and chapter 2 for discussions of the differences between tail and internal recursion.)

For reasons of style, we use tail recursion in Logo to accomplish sequential looping through data structures. For example, if you want to print the square root of each number in a list, you can write a nonrecursive procedure using the Logo primitive **SQRT**:

```
TO SQUAREROOTS1 :NUMBERS
LABEL "LOOP
IF EMPTYP :NUMBERS [STOP]
PRINT SQRT FIRST :NUMBERS
MAKE "NUMBERS BUTFIRST :NUMBERS
GO "LOOP
END
```

Or you could write a recursive procedure that uses **SQRT** to do the same thing:

```
TO SQUAREROOTS2 :NUMBERS
IF EMPTYP :NUMBERS [STOP]
PRINT SQRT FIRST :NUMBERS
SQUAREROOTS2 BUTFIRST :NUMBERS
END
```

Both of these procedures are used in the same way with a list of numbers
as input:

```
SQUAREROOTS1 [1 2 3 4]
SQUAREROOTS2 [1 2 3 4]
```

The strength of the second procedure is that it is more compact and
elegant. Recursion lets you feed the **BUTFIRST** of the list directly back
into the procedure for further processing. If you use **GO "LOOP**,
however, you must first assign a new value to a variable and then you
must loop back.

Lists can also be used much as structured records are used in Pascal
and C. This use involves extensive internal recursion: the structure of the
lists is itself internally recursive. This type of problem is discussed in
some detail in chapters 5, 6, and 7.

Selecting Particular List Elements

The one advantage that arrays have over lists is that arrays allow the
substitution of members at arbitrary positions in the sequence. Although
in chapter 4 you will find procedures to insert arbitrary items into a list,
they are much slower than a corresponding action on an array. Both
Apple Logo and Dr. Logo, however, have a primitive, **ITEM**, that re-
trieves an arbitrary item in a list. **ITEM** can be used to get at the *n*th
element of a list. Thus, **ITEM 4 [A B C D E]** outputs a result of **D**, the
fourth item in the list.

ITEM can also be used to get at random elements in a list. The Logo
primitive **COUNT** can be used to find the length of a list. Once you know
how to find the length of a list, then you can define a procedure to pick
out a random element in a list:

```
TO RANDOMPICK :LIST
OUTPUT ITEM (RANDOM COUNT :LIST) + 1 :LIST
END
```

The output of **COUNT :LIST** is used to determine the bounds of the call to the random number generator (explained in more detail in chapter 1). You must add 1 to the random number to avoid trying to select **ITEM 0**, which would give you an error message. The result of the random-number primitive is used to determine which element to select out of the list. In this situation, **:LIST** is used twice, once as input to **COUNT** and once as input to **ITEM**.

If you are using a version of Logo that does not have a primitive to select the *n*th item in a list, you can use this procedure:

```
TO ITEM :NUMBER :LIST
IF :LIST = [] [OUTPUT []]
IF :NUMBER = 1 [OUTPUT FIRST :LIST]
OUTPUT ITEM :NUMBER - 1 BUTFIRST :LIST
END
```

This procedure steps through the list, checking to see if it is empty or if the number is down to 1 yet. Each time it goes around again, it reduces the original number by 1 and takes off the first member of the list with **BUTFIRST**. When the number has finally been reduced to 1, the first element of the list is output as the result of the procedure.

Sentence Generator

In the previous section we developed a procedure to pick out random elements from a list. This procedure can be used to create a system that composes English sentences of words picked from lists of words grouped together by syntactic category.

Let's start by defining a sentence as simply a noun and a verb. After we have explored the fundamental principles, we can elaborate upon this simple structure. We need a list of nouns and a list of verbs. Define these two global Logo variables:

```
MAKE "NOUNS [BIRDS DOGS FISH PEOPLE]
MAKE "VERBS [RUN JUMP SWIM TALK]
```

With these lists defined, we can write two procedures that select random elements from each:

```
TO NOUN
OUTPUT RANDOMPICK :NOUNS
END

TO VERB
OUTPUT RANDOMPICK :VERBS
END
```

Now we can define a procedure that uses the primitive **SENTENCE** to put the output of **NOUN** and **VERB** together:

```
TO SENTENCEMAKER
PRINT SENTENCE NOUN VERB
END
```

At this point, repeated calls to **SENTENCEMAKER** give results like this:

```
PEOPLE SWIM
FISH TALK
FISH JUMP
DOGS SWIM
```

Now that you get the basic idea, you can add a list of adjectives and a procedure to pick from that list:

```
MAKE "ADJECTIVES [BIG LITTLE GREEN RED]

TO ADJECTIVE
OUTPUT RANDOMPICK :ADJECTIVES
END
```

Now change **SENTENCEMAKER** to look like this:

```
TO SENTENCEMAKER2
PRINT (SENTENCE ADJECTIVE NOUN VERB)
END
```

Notice that **SENTENCE** must now have all its inputs enclosed in parentheses because there are more than two inputs. Going further in this direction, you could add lists of adverbs (for instance, *really* and *almost*) to the **SENTENCEMAKER** environment. (Each new list must also have an accompanying procedure that picks out random elements from the list.)

Or you might add an empty list or two as a twist in the adjective list so that sometimes the sentence will not have an adjective. The new adjective list might look like this:

```
MAKE "ADJECTIVES [BIG LITTLE GREEN RED []]
```

Now sometimes **RANDOMPICK** will pick out the empty list instead of an adjective. Using empty lists is an easy way to add variety to the sentences that you are producing.

You can see how you can elaborate upon this simple idea by adding new word lists and new procedures to pick from those lists. You can also modify the basic idea by using lists of phrases rather than just words. You can have a list of subjects, a list of predicates, and associated procedures:

```
MAKE "SUBJECTS [[THE QUICK BROWN FOX][OLD
MACDONALD][THE OLD GRAY MARE]]

TO SUBJECTS
OUTPUT RANDOMPICK :SUBJECTS
END

MAKE "PREDICATES [[JUMPED OVER THE LAZY DOG]
[HAD A FARM] [AIN'T WHAT SHE USED TO BE]]

TO PREDICATES
OUTPUT RANDOMPICK :PREDICATES
END
```

Then you can rewrite the main step in **SENTENCEMAKER2** to read

```
PRINT SENTENCE SUBJECT PREDICATE
```

You can also give **SENTENCEMAKER2** the ability to augment its word lists. You can write a short procedure that every so often asks the user to type a new word or phrase into one list or another. This way the program does not get boring quickly, and it grows with each use.

First, define a procedure to tell **SENTENCEMAKER2** when to learn new words:

```
TO HUNGRY.TO.LEARN :HOW.OFTEN
OUTPUT EQUALP RANDOM :HOW.OFTEN 0
END
```

This procedure takes a number as input and outputs **TRUE** or **FALSE**, depending on whether a call to **RANDOM** with that number is equal to 0. It uses the primitive **EQUALP** to check for the possible equality of 0 and **RANDOM :HOW.OFTEN**. Essentially, **EQUALP** returns **TRUE** once every **:HOW.OFTEN** times; thus, a call to **HUNGRY.TO.LEARN 5** outputs **TRUE** about once every five times. Because this procedure outputs **TRUE** or **FALSE**, it can be used as input to an **IF** command, as follows:

```
TO SENTENCEMAKER3
PRINT SENTENCE SUBJECT PREDICATE
IF HUNGRY.TO.LEARN 6 [GETNEW.PREDICATE]
IF HUNGRY.TO.LEARN 6 [GETNEW.SUBJECT]
SENTENCEMAKER3
END
```

The two procedures that are used to get new phrases are very similar to each other:

```
TO GETNEW.PREDICATE
PRINT []
PRINT [TYPE IN A NEW PREDICATE...]
MAKE "PREDICATES FPUT READLIST :PREDICATES
END

TO GETNEW.SUBJECT
PRINT []
PRINT [TYPE IN A NEW SUBJECT...]
MAKE "SUBJECTS FPUT READLIST :SUBJECTS
END
```

These two procedures use **FPUT** to add the new phrase typed in by the user (**READLIST**) to the global value of the appropriate list. Now when you use **SENTENCEMAKER3** it will ask you sometimes for a new subject, sometimes for a new predicate, and sometimes for both. If you want it to ask more or less often, change the number given to **HUNGRY.TO.LEARN** as input. As it is written right now, it will ask about every sixth time around.

These projects give just a glimmer of the purposes for which you can use lists in Logo. They do, however, touch on some of the fundamental things that you can do, such as creating global lists, picking out selected items, adding user input to lists, recursively stepping through lists, and using lists of numbers. The rest of this chapter will explore the arithmetic capabilities of Logo in more detail. Chapters 4 through 7 discuss in much greater depth the uses of lists in Logo to structure data and guide program flow.

USING MATHEMATICS ───────────────────────────

You have already seen in this and other chapters that Logo can perform the basic math functions: adding, subtracting, multiplying, and dividing. In chapter 1 there are some turtle graphics procedures that use the trigonometric functions available in Logo. In this section we shall take a closer look at some projects using Logo's math functions.

Prefix and Infix Notation ──────────────────────────

Logo allows both *prefix* and *infix* notation for expressing math functions. To write an expression that adds 3 and 4, you can use either of the following:

```
3 + 4        infix notation
SUM 3 4      prefix notation
```

One advantage of prefix notation is that it requires fewer parentheses to produce unambiguous expressions. Consider the expression

```
(5 * (6 + (7 * (32 + 8))) + 12
```

It can be written in prefix form as follows:

```
SUM 12 PRODUCT 5 SUM 6 PRODUCT 7 SUM 32 8
```

Prefix form takes some getting used to, but it is easy to grasp if you learn to evaluate it from right to left, working backward toward the beginning of the expression. In fact, most complex Logo statements are best evaluated from back to front. This is because often the input to the first statements must be produced by statements toward the end of the line.

This section will not attempt to cover all the math functions available in Logo, but it will cover a few projects that illustrate some strategies for writing mathematical procedures in Logo.

Logical Operations

Logo allows you to combine predicate expressions that output **TRUE** or **FALSE** into a single predicate value. For example, if you are moving the turtle around and want it to stop if the *x* coordinate is greater than 100 or the *y* coordinate is less than 0, you write this Logo expression:

```
IF OR (XCOR > 100) (YCOR < 0) [STOP]
```

OR is a Logo primitive that takes two or more predicates as input, analyzes them as parts of a logical *or* expression, and outputs **TRUE** or **FALSE**. If at least one of the inputs is true, then the whole expression is true. Notice that **OR** is a prefix operator and that its inputs are written after it.

Logo can also take two or more predicates and analyze them as parts of a logical *and* expression, as shown here:

```
IF AND (:TODAY = "FRIDAY) (:TIME > 5) [GET.DOWN]
```

All the inputs must be true for an **AND** expression to be true.

Finally, Logo can analyze the logical opposite of a predicate with the primitive **NOT**. This command takes one input and returns the opposite logical value:

```
IF NOT :NUMBER > 100 [GO.ON]
```

These functions are much the same as corresponding operations in other computer languages, except that the prefix notation may seem somewhat artificial to you at first. You may find yourself tempted to write **XCOR > 100 OR YCOR < 0**. Just remember that logical operators in Logo are like most other Logo functions: their inputs follow them.

Temperature Conversion

First, imagine a procedure that takes in a number representing the temperature in degrees Fahrenheit and outputs a number representing the temperature in degrees Celsius. Almost everyone has learned (and subsequently forgotten) the formula to convert Fahrenheit values to Celsius values:

Celsius = 5 × (Fahrenheit − 32)/9

On the basis of this formula it is easy to create a procedure to perform the conversion:

```
TO F.TO.C :DEGREES.F
OUTPUT (5 * (:DEGREES.F - 32)) / 9
END
```

To use **F.TO.C**, give it the temperature in Fahrenheit, and it outputs the temperature in Celsius. Because it only outputs the answer, you must use it with **PRINT** or as input to another procedure or primitive:

```
PRINT F.TO.C 212
PRINT F.TO.C 32
PRINT F.TO.C 100
```

This procedure uses infix notation and parentheses because there are no Logo prefix primitives for division or subtraction. But we can define our own prefix procedures for them:

```
TO DIV :NUM1 :NUM2
OUTPUT :NUM1 / :NUM2
END
```

```
TO SUB :NUM1 :NUM2
OUTPUT :NUM1 - :NUM2
END
```

Now the conversion procedure can be written with prefix notation:

```
TO F.TO.C.PREFIX :DEGREES.F
OUTPUT DIV TIMES 5 SUB :DEGREES.F 32 9
END
```

The method you use is mostly a matter of personal style. The nice thing about Logo is that it gives you the flexibility to customize the language to fit your own style. Now, given the formula for converting Celsius to Fahrenheit, you should be able to write your own procedure:

Fahrenheit = (9 × Celsius/5) + 32

Euclid's Greatest Common Factor

Next, consider Euclid's algorithm for finding the greatest common factor (GCF) of two numbers. First, if one of the numbers is 0, then the GCF is the other number. If neither of the numbers is 0, then divide the second number by the first, take the remainder of that division, and try to find the GCF of the remainder and the first number. This process is repeated until one of the numbers is 0.

We can use the Logo primitive **REMAINDER** to give the integer remainder of a division of two numbers. For example, **REMAINDER 7 2** outputs **1**. The second number is divided into the first, and the remainder of that division is the output of **REMAINDER**.

The procedure to figure out the greatest common factor involves two inputs and uses tail recursion to repeat until one of the numbers is 0, at which point it outputs the other number. Notice that each time through, the second number is dropped and replaced by the first number. The first number is replaced by the remainder of the division of the first and second numbers. Here again, tail recursion and inputs make it unnecessary to assign values to temporary variables before looping around again. Rather, the output of **REMAINDER :NUM1 :NUM2** is used directly in place of the first input in the recursive call to **GCF**:

```
TO GCF :NUM1 :NUM2
IF :NUM1 = 0 [OUTPUT :NUM2]
OUTPUT GCF (REMAINDER :NUM2 :NUM1) :NUM1
END
```

Once this procedure is defined, you can use it to find the greatest common factor of two numbers, as in

```
PRINT GCF 4 8
PRINT GCF 249 77
PRINT GCF 32 0
```

In the original discussion of Euclid's algorithm, we said that if either of the numbers is 0, then the GCF is the other number, yet you might notice that our procedure checks only the first number. In a case where the second number is 0, as in the last example above, the procedure calls itself recursively one time. The second time through, the first input will be 0, as a result of taking the remainder of 32 and 0, and the second input will be 32. At this point 32 will be output as the GCF. You could instead write a procedure to check both numbers each time through, but since a 0 in the second place is always caught after only one recursive cycle, it is probably not worthwhile to check both numbers every time. In any event, checking only the first input gives a simpler procedure.

Instead of using **GCF** with the **PRINT** command, you can use it in a project that requires the greatest common factor of two numbers. Once it is defined, **GCF** can be used just like any other math function in Logo. By defining math functions this way, you can create a custom math language for any sort of application.

Fibonacci Numbers

Next, consider the famed Fibonacci numbers:

0, 1, 1, 2, 3, 5, 8, 13, 21, 34, 55, 89, 144, . . .

The next number in the series is always obtained by adding the previous two numbers, starting with 0 and 1. This series can be neatly defined with the list operators and math functions of Logo. The procedure keeps the growing Fibonacci series in a list. We must seed the list with the first two numbers, 0 and 1. We also need some sort of check step to stop the recursion. Let's have the procedure stop when the largest number in the series is greater than 1,000:

```
TO FIB :SERIES
IF LAST :SERIES > 1000 [OUTPUT :SERIES]
OUTPUT FIB LPUT SUM (LAST :SERIES)
                   (LAST BUTLAST :SERIES)
               :SERIES
END
```

FIB uses **SUM** to add the last number of the series to the next-to-last number (**LAST BUTLAST**). That sum is then **LPUT** onto the series, and the procedure cycles again with the new series as input. Each time through, the list of numbers grows by one member, with the new number tacked on the end. This new number is then used to compute the next number in the series. This process continues until the last number is greater than 1,000, at which point the entire series is output. Try it now by calling **FIB** with a seed list:

```
PRINT FIB [0 1]
```

Rather than trying to remember what the seed is every time you use **FIB**, you might want to write a little shell around **FIB** to supply the seed list for you:

```
TO FIBONACCI
OUTPUT FIB [0 1]
END
```

Once again, as with the previous example, you can use the output of **FIBONACCI** directly with **PRINT**, or you can feed it into some other procedure that requires a Fibonacci series. An example of such a procedure is one that computes the ratios of adjacent Fibonacci numbers and puts the results into a list. As you go through the Fibonacci numbers, the ratio of any two adjacent numbers approaches a constant value that is the same as the ratio between the sides of the golden rectangle of ancient Greece. (For a more complete discussion of the golden rectangle and Fibonacci numbers, see David Thornburg's excellent book, *Discovering Apple Logo*, listed in Appendix D.)

```
TO RATIOS :LIST
IF EMPTYP BUTFIRST :LIST [OUTPUT []]   ;ONLY 1 LEFT
OUTPUT FPUT (FIRST :LIST) / (FIRST BUTFIRST :LIST)
              RATIOS BUTFIRST :LIST
END
```

Given a list of numbers, **RATIOS** divides the first two members and computes their ratio. This ratio is **FPUT** into the eventual result of the entire ratio series. For now, the result of that division is left hanging until the rest of the ratios are computed, Next, the first member of the input list is taken off with **BUTFIRST**, and the new list is sent around again to find more ratios. This continues until there is only one member left (**EMPTYP BUTFIRST**), at which point an empty list is output. This empty list then becomes the depository for all the accumulated ratios that have been computed and are waiting for something to be **FPUT** into.

Figure 3.2 shows the flow of the procedure as it processes a short list of numbers. The recursion goes downward, reducing the input list by one member each time until there is only one member left, and then the empty list works its way back up, collecting ratios and **FPUT**ting them into an output list. The figure shows how the ratios computed at each level are left hanging until the recursion bottoms out and then comes back up to collect them. The first ratio computed is the last one to be **FPUT** into the output list. This is a rather subtle recursive strategy that

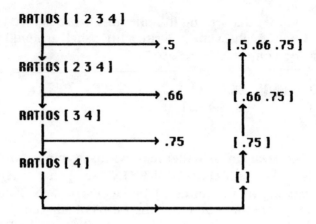

Figure 3.2
The flow of RATIOS

is discussed and developed more completely in chapter 4. For now, suffice to say that the list that is produced has the ratio of the first two numbers of the input list as its first member, and the ratio of the last two members (assuming an even number of members) as its last member.

Now if you use the output of **FIBONACCI** as the input to **RATIOS**, you can type in something like this:

```
PRINT RATIOS FIBONACCI
```

When you do this you get a list of decimal numbers several lines long. At best, it is hard to read. But since the output of **RATIOS** is a list, why not feed it into **PRETTYPRINT**, which we defined earlier in the chapter? **PRETTYPRINT**, which probably seemed trivial at the time, comes in handy now to take each of the numbers in the output list of **RATIOS** and put it on a separate line. Use it by typing

```
PRETTYPRINT RATIOS FIBONACCI
```

This example shows how the output from one procedure can be used as the input to another procedure whose input in turn can be used as input to still another procedure. This is the essence of a good Logo procedure. Now you see why it is a good idea to write procedures that **OUTPUT** their results rather than **PRINT** them. If you want to see the results on the screen, you can always feed the output to **PRINT**. Writing procedures that use **OUTPUT** gives you flexibility to use your procedures for a wide range of applications.

This example also shows how numbers in lists can be manipulated by the basic list commands. Numbers can be taken out, computed, and then recombined into new lists with many of the same commands as are used to work with words in lists.

SUMMARY

The projects in this chapter have introduced the fundamental operations that Logo uses to manipulate text and numbers. One of the nicest aspects of Logo is that it allows you to manipulate words, lists, and numbers with the same commands. This symmetry allows for consistent problem-solving strategies.

These projects also show how you can use tail recursion to iterate an operation through a list of data, operating on each member in turn. This is a fundamental Logo control strategy, and it can be applied to many different kinds of problems.

The projects in the remaining chapters will go into these topics—words, lists, and numbers—in greater detail and depth. You are encouraged to try your own projects using the Logo primitives outlined here and also to read through the glossary at the end of the book (Appendix E) to find commands that are not discussed in the text but that might help you solve your particular problem.

Logo is meant to be an exploratory tool, so be adventurous. It is often said that if you aren't making mistakes, you probably aren't learning. The best way to learn Logo is to go through the examples in this and other books, imagine your own problems, and work until you have solved them.

4 LIST TOOLS

ADD

DELETE

REPLACE

MAP and MAPOP

Sorting

Summary

This chapter will show you how to use some of the list primitives that were explained in previous chapters. In particular, here we shall develop a set of tools to modify lists of data. These tools make extensive use of the **OUTPUT** primitive. They take a list as input, make a copy of it, modify its structure somewhat, and then output the modified copy when they finish execution. They do not change the global value of the input list unless you expressly ask them to by feeding their output to a **MAKE** expression. This absence of unplanned side effects is one of the strengths of the **OUTPUT** primitive. Because the procedures developed here simply output a value when they are done, they can be used in a variety of situations (hence their designation *tools*). These tools also make extensive use of recursion and thus are models for other tools that you may wish to develop in the course of your Logo explorations.

First of all, we need a list to operate on throughout the rest of the chapter. It should be made up of words and numbers and other lists, just to make sure that our tools can handle a variety of forms. Type in the following definition:

```
MAKE "SAMPLE [A B CAT [D E] 1 2 [A [B]] A B]
```

Notice that some members of this list occur more than once. The list has nine members: **A**, **B**, **CAT**, **[D E]**, **1**, **2**, **[A [B]]**, **A**, and **B**. Before the end of this chapter you may come to know this list very well.

ADD

First we want to be able to add a member to a list. We can call the relevant procedure **ADD**. It needs two inputs, an item to add and a list to add the item to:

```
TO ADD :ITEM :LIST
OUTPUT FPUT :ITEM :LIST
END
```

This procedure is very simple—actually, trivial. It just **FPUT**s the **:ITEM** onto the **:LIST** and **OUTPUT**s the result. You could use **LPUT** instead of **FPUT**, but **LPUT** is noticeably slower than **FPUT**, especially with longer lists. You might also consider using **LIST** or **SENTENCE** to combine the new element into the list, but neither is appropriate for this procedure. In particular, if you use **LIST** instead of **FPUT**, then **ADD "FOO :SAMPLE** gives **[FOO [A B CAT [D E] 1 2 [A [B]] A B]]**.

If you use **SENTENCE** instead of **FPUT**, then **ADD** "**FOO :SAMPLE** gives [FOO A B CAT [D E] 1 2 [A [B]] A B], which is okay. But if you try **ADD [FOO] :SAMPLE**, you also get **[FOO A B CAT [D E] 1 2 [A [B]] A B]**. **SENTENCE** fails to maintain the distinction between a list added to a list and a word added to a list.

Now let's try out the **ADD** procedure:

```
PRINT ADD "FOO :SAMPLE
```

This gives you

```
FOO A B CAT [D E] 1 2 [A [B]] A B
```

If you say

```
PRINT ADD [FOO] :SAMPLE
```

you see

```
[FOO] A B CAT [D E] 1 2 [A [B]] A B
```

Notice, however, that if you now say

```
PRINT :SAMPLE
```

you get the original value of the list:

```
A B CAT [D E] 1 2 [A [B]] A B
```

It is important for you to realize that these tool procedures do not change the value of the lists that are given to them as input. They merely output a modified *copy* of that input. If you wish to change the value of a list, you must do it with the **MAKE** command, as in

```
MAKE "SAMPLE ADD "BAR :SAMPLE
```

In this case, the output of **ADD** is used by the **MAKE** command to assign a new value to "**SAMPLE**. Now if you type

```
PRINT :SAMPLE
```

you get

```
BAR A B CAT [D E] 1 2 [A [B]] A B
```

DELETE

Now that we can add an item to our list, we want to be able to delete any item. This procedure needs two inputs also, an item to be deleted and a list from which to delete it:

```
TO DELETE :ITEM :LIST
IF EMPTYP :LIST
     [OUTPUT :LIST]
IF EQUALP FIRST :LIST :ITEM
     [OUTPUT BUTFIRST :LIST]
OUTPUT FPUT FIRST :LIST
           DELETE :ITEM BUTFIRST :LIST
```

This procedure first checks to see if the list that it was given as input is empty. If the list is empty, there is nothing to delete, so the procedure just stops and outputs the empty list. Remember that when a procedure has something definite to output, execution stops and the procedure returns control to whatever called it in the first place.

If the list is not empty, then **DELETE** goes on to see if the first element of the list is equal to the item that is to be deleted. If the first element of the list is to be deleted, then the output of the procedure is the **BUTFIRST** of the list. Once again, there is a definite object to output, so the procedure stops and passes this object back to its caller. This is pretty straightforward. If the list is not empty, and if the first element of the list is not the one to be deleted, however, the next step gets a little tricky: the output of **DELETE** becomes the first element of the list combined with the output of **DELETE** using the **BUTFIRST** of the list. **FPUT** is used to combine the first element with the eventual output of

```
DELETE :ITEM BUTFIRST :LIST
```

DELETE calls itself recursively, checking the first element of a diminishing list each time it goes through until either it finds the element to be deleted or the list is empty.

DELETE keeps cycling until it finds something immediate to output instead of the recursive call in the last line. An example with a short list will illustrate. Imagine a list **[A B C D E F]**. A call to

```
DELETE "D [A B C D E F]
```

leads to the steps shown in figure 4.1. You can see that as **DELETE** goes down through its first three levels of recursion it outputs the first member of the list and goes on to check the rest of the list. The single members are left hanging until the deepest level of recursion is finished. Then they are picked up as the procedure backs out of the recursive hole it has dug.

This type of recursion works like a mine-shaft elevator that lets workers off at each level of the mine as it goes down to the bottom. When the elevator reaches the bottom and starts back up, the last workers off are the first ones picked up. As you follow the arrows back up from the fourth level in figure 4.1, you can see how the individual members that have been accumulating are **FPUT** into the output list.

If the list is longer, the first elements just continue to be successively lined up (to await placement in the output list) until one of the two stop conditions is met. If the targeted item is never found, then the queue of elements is just put into an empty list, and the resulting output is exactly the same as the input. As with most recursive procedures, the process can be subtle, so take some time to think about it. Try walking through the steps with some lists of your own. This process of accumulating items to be output into a final list will be used many times throughout the rest of this book. Make sure you understand it thoroughly.

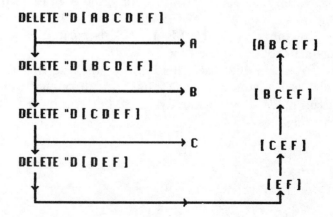

Figure 4.1
DELETE

In the last section, we changed the value of **:SAMPLE** by adding **"BAR** to it (**MAKE "SAMPLE ADD "BAR :SAMPLE**). Now let's change it back to its original value:

```
MAKE "SAMPLE DELETE "BAR :SAMPLE
```

Now when you type **PRINT :SAMPLE** you should get

```
A B CAT [D E] 1 2 [A [B]] A B
```

There is a slight bug in this procedure as now written. If you use **DELETE** with **:SAMPLE**, as in

```
PRINT DELETE "A :SAMPLE
```

you get

```
B CAT [D E] 1 2 [A [B]] A B
```

The first **"A** is taken out, but you can see that the other **"A** toward the end of the list is not deleted. This is because **DELETE** cycles through the list only until the first time it finds the item it is supposed to delete. If that item occurs more than once, **DELETE** does not find its second and succeeding occurrences. (Of course the **A** in **[A [B]]** shouldn't be taken out: it is not a member of **:SAMPLE** but rather a member of a sublist that is a member of **:SAMPLE**. **[A [B]]** is treated as a unit when matched against the item to be deleted.)

You can eliminate this bug by ensuring that the procedure always calls itself recursively until it has gone through the entire list. This makes it run more slowly in many cases, but you have to weigh speed against thoroughness.

```
TO DELETE.ALL :ITEM :LIST
IF EMPTYP :LIST
     [OUTPUT :LIST]
IF EQUALP FIRST :LIST :ITEM
     [OUTPUT DELETE.ALL :ITEM BUTFIRST :LIST]
OUTPUT FPUT FIRST :LIST
          DELETE.ALL :ITEM BUTFIRST :LIST
END
```

The only real change here from **DELETE** is in what happens when there is a match between the first item of the list and the item to be deleted. Compare this line with its counterpart in **DELETE**. In **DELETE**, the item was simply lopped off the list with **BUTFIRST**, and the rest of the list was **OUTPUT**. Here, the item is taken off with **BUTFIRST**, but the rest of the list is fed back to **DELETE.ALL** for further checking. The only case that results in an **OUTPUT** and does not involve recursion is the case of the empty list. With this procedure you know that all the members of the list have been checked.

REPLACE

Now that we can add and delete items from a list, we can also develop a way to replace certain items in a list. This procedure takes three inputs: an old item to be replaced, a new item to replace it, and a particular list. **REPLACE** is very similar to **DELETE** in the way that it looks at the first element of the list and, if necessary, cycles recursively:

```
TO REPLACE :OLD.ITEM :NEW.ITEM :LIST
IF EMPTYP :LIST
      [OUTPUT :LIST]
IF EQUALP FIRST :LIST :OLD.ITEM
      [OUTPUT FPUT :NEW.ITEM BUTFIRST :LIST]
OUTPUT FPUT FIRST :LIST
               REPLACE :OLD.ITEM
                       :NEW.ITEM
                       BUTFIRST :LIST
```

This procedure goes through the list one member at a time, checking to see if the list is empty or if the first member of the list is the one to be replaced. When it finds the item to be replaced, it removes that item with **BUTFIRST :LIST** and outputs the new item grafted into the **BUTFIRST** of the list with **FPUT**. Figure 4.2 shows how the output of **REPLACE** is accumulated down through the levels of recursion and then picked up and reassembled into the final output list. Try **REPLACE** now with

```
PRINT REPLACE [D E] "NEW.WORD :SAMPLE
```

which gives you

```
A B CAT NEW.WORD 1 2 [A [B]] A B
```

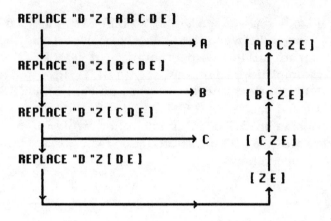

Figure 4.2
REPLACE

Notice, of course, that the global value of **SAMPLE** is not changed:
PRINT :SAMPLE still gives

```
A B CAT [D E] 1 2 [A [B]] A B
```

This procedure has the same bug that we saw in **DELETE**, namely
that it finds only the first occurrence of a targeted item in a list. The
solution to the problem is very similar to adding **DELETE.ALL**, with the
same overhead of additional, perhaps unnecessary, recursion:

```
TO REPLACE.ALL :OLD.ITEM :NEW.ITEM :LIST
IF EMPTYP :LIST
     [OUTPUT :LIST]
IF EQUALP FIRST :LIST :OLD.ITEM
     [OUTPUT FPUT :NEW.ITEM
                   REPLACE.ALL :OLD.ITEM
                               :NEW.ITEM
                               BUTFIRST :LIST
     ]
OUTPUT FPUT FIRST :LIST
           REPLACE.ALL :OLD.ITEM
                       :NEW.ITEM
                       BUTFIRST :LIST
END
```

In this procedure you can see that if the first item in a list is the "**OLD.ITEM** to be replaced, then it is dropped, the "**NEW.ITEM** is put in its place, and the rest of the list is checked for more occurrences of the "**OLD.ITEM**. When the first item of the list is not the "**OLD.ITEM**, then the first item is retained, and the rest of the list is checked for the "**OLD.ITEM**. When all the members of the list have been checked, the procedure finally outputs the empty list, which is then filled with the waiting queue of retained and replaced members. Now if you try

```
MAKE "SAMPLE REPLACE.ALL "A "Z :SAMPLE
```

and

```
PRINT :SAMPLE
```

you see

```
Z B CAT [D E] 1 2 [A [B]] Z B
```

Then try

```
PRINT REPLACE.ALL 1 "ONE :SAMPLE
```

which gives

```
Z B CAT [D E] ONE 2 [A [B]] Z B
```

There is one more thing you might want to change. As written now, neither **REPLACE** nor **REPLACE.ALL** inserts the "**NEW.ITEM** in the list if the "**OLD.ITEM** is not a member of the list. In some situations, you might want to check a list for a certain item and replace it if it is there, or add the new item if the old item is not there. A notable example of such a situation is discussed in Appendix C: when property lists are being updated, an old property listing should be replaced by the new version. If a property is not already listed, however, then the new listing should be added.

The change needed is very simple. When **REPLACE** goes through the whole list and does not find the **OLD.ITEM**, it outputs an empty list that then picks up the accumulated output of the previous recursive levels. Our new procedure instead outputs a list containing the

NEW.ITEM whenever it goes through the whole list without finding the **OLD.ITEM**. The **NEW.ITEM** must be output as a list because the other members of the original list, which are waiting in a line, must themselves be **FPUT** into a list. Simply outputting the **NEW.ITEM** as a word results in an error message.

```
TO REPLACE.OR.ADD :OLD.ITEM :NEW.ITEM :LIST
IF EMPTYP :LIST
    [OUTPUT (LIST :NEW.ITEM)]
IF EQUALP FIRST :LIST :OLD.ITEM
    [OUTPUT FPUT :NEW.ITEM BUTFIRST :LIST]
OUTPUT FPUT FIRST :LIST
            REPLACE.OR.ADD :OLD.ITEM
                           :NEW.ITEM
                           BUTFIRST :LIST
END
```

The parentheses around **(LIST :NEW.ITEM)** are necessary because **LIST** usually takes two inputs, and here it is getting only one.

Because we want the **NEW.ITEM** output at the end only if the procedure has gone through the whole list without finding the **OLD.ITEM**, we have modified **REPLACE**, rather than **REPLACE.ALL**, to get **REPLACE.OR.ADD**. **REPLACE.ALL**, because of its relentless recursion, always ends up emptying the list, but **REPLACE** and **REPLACE.OR.ADD** empty the list only when the **OLD.ITEM** cannot be found.

MAP AND MAPOP ─────────────────────────────

The next two tools differ from the ones that have come before in that they do not alter the lists given to them as input. These procedures allow you to perform any particular operation on a whole list of objects. The original list is not disturbed. **MAP** and **MAPOP** are written to mimic the action of the LISP function **MAPCAR**.

Suppose you have a list of numbers, and you want to get the square root of each number. Without using **MAPOP**, you can write a short looping routine to take the numbers out of the list one by one and put their square roots into an output list:

```
TO SQUAREROOTS :LIST
IF EMPTYP :LIST
     [OUTPUT :LIST]
OUTPUT FPUT SQRT FIRST :LIST
             SQUAREROOTS BUTFIRST :LIST
END
```

You can probably see that the structure of this procedure is similar to the structure of the other tools we have developed in this chapter. Since **SQUAREROOTS** only produces an output list, it must be used with some other operation, as in

```
PRINT SQUAREROOTS [1 2 3 4]
```

which (depending on the way your version of Logo handles floating-point numbers) produces something like

```
1 1.4142135623731 1.7320508075688 2
```

This procedure isn't difficult to use, but it is tedious: you have to do a separate looping procedure for every new operation that you want to apply to a list. **MAPOP**, in contrast, is a general-purpose tool that takes the name of a procedure or primitive and a list of inputs, applies the operation to each member of the list, and outputs a list of the results:

```
TO MAPOP :PROCEDURE :LIST
IF EMPTYP :LIST
     [OUTPUT []]
OUTPUT (FPUT RUN SENTENCE :PROCEDURE
                          QWOTE FIRST :LIST
             MAPOP :PROCEDURE BUTFIRST :LIST
        )
END
```

The structure of this procedure is very similar to the structure of **SQUAREROOTS**. The key statement is

```
OUTPUT (FPUT RUN SENTENCE :PROCEDURE
                          QWOTE FIRST :LIST
             MAPOP :PROCEDURE BUTFIRST :LIST
        )
```

The output of this step is an **FPUT** statement. The two inputs to **FPUT** are the outcome of **RUN**ning the **:PROCEDURE** with the first element of the **:LIST** as input, and the output of **MAPOP** with the rest of the list. **RUN** is a primitive that takes a list of instructions as input and executes the instructions listed. **RUN** is an important primitive in Logo, allowing Logo to manipulate data and instructions in exactly the same way. In this case, **SENTENCE** is used to combine the procedure name given to **MAPOP** as input, held in the variable **:PROCEDURE**, into a list with **QWOTE FIRST :LIST**. **QWOTE** is required to put quotation marks before, or another set of list brackets around, the proposed input to **PROCEDURE**:

```
TO QWOTE :INPUT
IF WORDP :INPUT
    [OUTPUT WORD "" :INPUT]
    [OUTPUT (LIST :INPUT)]
END
```

If you use

```
QWOTE FIRST [A B C]
```

then the output is "**A**. If you use

```
QWOTE FIRST [[A B] C D]
```

then the output is **[[AB]]**.

So now if we want to go back to our original example to take the square roots of listed numbers, we can type

```
PRINT MAPOP "SQRT [1 2 3 4]
```

and get

```
1 1.4142135623731 1.73258756888 2
```

Notice that the name of the procedure is preceded by quotation marks when it is used as input to **MAPOP**. If the procedure name were not thus marked, the procedure itself would be executed, and its name would not be fed to **MAPOP**.

This works just fine as long as the procedure that you are using is one that only **OUTPUT**s. In LISP, from which this procedure is derived, all primitives and procedures output their result. In Logo there are primitives and procedures that do not output a result, but rather do something, such as draw on the graphics screen. Clearly, **MAPOP** does not work in this next example:

```
MAPOP "SETPOS [[0 0] [120 -34] [-120 120]]
```

There is no need to keep a list of output here because there is no output from **SETPOS**. If you give this instruction, Logo complains that there is no output. Instead of using **MAPOP**, you want to just **RUN** the procedure with the first input from the list, then go around and **RUN** it again with the next input from the list, and so on until the list is empty. With this in mind, you can write the following procedure:

```
TO MAP :PROCEDURE :LIST
IF EMPTYP :LIST
      [STOP]
RUN SENTENCE :PROCEDURE QWOTE FIRST :LIST
MAP :PROCEDURE BUTFIRST :LIST
END
```

You can see that **MAP** is similar to but simpler than **MAPOP**. Its syntax for use is the same as for **MAPOP**. You say

```
MAP "SETPOS [[0 0] [120 -34] [-120 120]]
```

You will find that you can use **MAPOP** or **MAP** instead of writing short loops to go through a list and do the same thing to each element.

SORTING

In many situations it is valuable to be able to sort a list of data into some kind of order. It seems natural, for instance, to sort a list of numbers into ascending order, with the smallest number first. We can use Logo to define recursive procedures that sort in this way. Actually, Dr. Logo has a primitive that sorts lists of numbers or words. This primitive, because it is implemented in machine code, runs many times faster than anything we can define in Logo. So the sorting routines developed here are of only academic interest to you if you are using Dr. Logo or some other version of Logo that includes sorting primitives. If you are using Apple Logo, you do not have sorting primitives at your disposal, so these procedures are useful to you.

Two kinds of sorting will be discussed in this section, *insert sorting* and *merge sorting*. A third kind, *tree sorting*, which is not available as a primitive in any version of Logo, is discussed in chapter 6.

INSORT ————————————————————————————

Consider the list of unordered numbers **[56 31 2 45 101 0 23]**. To sort these numbers into ascending order, you can take them one at a time and insert them into the proper place in another, already sorted, list. Instead of trying to sort the whole list at once, think about sorting its members just one at a time.

The procedure for inserting a number into an already sorted list has to go through the sorted list one element at a time and check each element against the item to be inserted. The procedure keeps checking until it finds an item in the sorted list that is greater in value than the item to be inserted. The new item is inserted into the list before the item greater in value, and the new list is output:

```
TO INSERT :NUMBER :LIST
IF EMPTYP :LIST
      [OUTPUT (LIST :NUMBER)]
IF :NUMBER < FIRST :LIST
      [OUTPUT FPUT :NUMBER :LIST]    ; INSERT HERE
      [OUTPUT FPUT FIRST :LIST    ; KEEP LOOKING
                      INSERT :NUMBER
                          BUTFIRST :LIST
         ]
END
```

This procedure accumulates the members of the list with **FPUT** until one is found that is greater in value than the item to be inserted. At that point the new item is grafted onto the remaining members of the list, and then the accumulated members of the list, which had been passed over, are put back into the list with the waiting **FPUT** commands. This method of combining **FPUT** with recursive calls is a variation of the technique used in other tools in this chapter. Figure 4.3 shows diagrammatically how the waiting outputs are combined as the procedure backs out of its recursive calls.

Once you can insert a single item into a sorted list, then the task of sorting a list of numbers boils down to simply going through the list and inserting the numbers one by one into an already sorted list. The trick is to use the empty list as the original sorted destination list and insert the

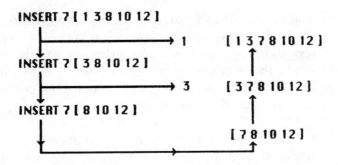

Figure 4.3
INSERT

last element into it. Then the next-to-last element is inserted into the list resulting from the first insertion. This process of backing up through a list suggests that recursion is involved in the solution:

```
TO INSORT :LIST
IF EMPTYP :LIST
     [OUTPUT []]
OUTPUT INSERT FIRST :LIST
               INSORT BUTFIRST :LIST
END
```

If you study this procedure you will see that it repeats recursively until the list is empty and then backs up and inserts the last element, then the next-to-last, and so on until the first element is finally inserted. At every step of the way back out, the destination list is already sorted, because it begins as an empty list and each subsequent insertion leaves it still sorted. You can try it out by typing

```
PRINT INSORT [3 6 1 10 9 7]
```

or some such command. Like the other tools developed in this chapter, **INSORT** does not alter the value of the list that is given to it for input. It merely outputs a sorted copy of the list, which you may use as you see fit. If you want to change the value of the input list, then you must use **MAKE**, as in

```
MAKE "NUMBERS [34 56 21 33 2 98]
MAKE "NUMBERS INSORT :NUMBERS
PRINT :NUMBERS
```

You can adapt this procedure to work with lists of words, also: just change the test used to control insertion in the list. With numbers, we use the *less than* sign (<), a Logo primitive. With words, we define a procedure that determines when one word is in some sense *less than* another word. First we must decide under what circumstances one word is to be considered less than another word:

1 If a longer word begins with the characters that make up a shorter word (and the positions of the characters are the same in both words), then the shorter word is less than the longer word. For instance, **CAT** is less than **CATTLE**.

2 Words starting with letters close to the beginning of the alphabet are less than words starting with letters not as close to the beginning of the alphabet. If the first letters are the same, then the second letters are compared, and so on: **CAT** is less than **DOG**, and **CAB** is less than **CAT**.

From these rules, we can define a procedure:

```
TO LESS.THAN :WORD1 :WORD2
IF EMPTYP :WORD1
    [OUTPUT "TRUE]    ; WORD1 SHORTER
IF EMPTYP :WORD2
    [OUTPUT "FALSE]    ; WORD2 SHORTER
IF ASCII FIRST :WORD1 < ASCII FIRST :WORD2
    [OUTPUT "TRUE]
IF ASCII FIRST :WORD1 > ASCII FIRST :WORD2
    [OUTPUT "FALSE]
; SO FAR THE SAME, CHECK THE REST
OUTPUT LESS.THAN BUTFIRST :WORD1
               BUTFIRST :WORD2
END
```

This procedure is rather straightforward. It uses the primitive **ASCII** to get the American Standard Code for Information Interchange (ASCII) code (used by the computer to identify characters) for the first character of each word. A lower ASCII code means a letter closer to the beginning of the alphabet. You should notice, however, that this procedure actually tests for the condition *less than or equal to* because of the way that it checks whether one word is shorter than the other. For the purposes of sorting, however, the test for the condition *less than or equal to* works just fine, so we can leave it as it is.

Now if we use this new test in the insert procedure, we get a new procedure, **INSERT.WORD**:

```
TO INSERT.WORD :WORD :LIST
IF EMPTYP :LIST
     [OUTPUT (LIST :WORD)]
IF LESS.THAN :WORD FIRST :LIST    ; NOTE CHANGE
     [OUTPUT FPUT :WORD :LIST]    ; INSERT HERE
     [OUTPUT FPUT FIRST :LIST     ; KEEP LOOKING
                     INSERT.WORD :WORD
                              BUTFIRST :LIST

     ]
END
```

With this change made, we can now define a modified **INSORT** called **WORDSORT**:

```
TO WORDSORT :LIST
IF EMPTYP :LIST
     [OUTPUT []]
OUTPUT INSERT.WORD FIRST :LIST
                WORDSORT BUTFIRST :LIST
END
```

You can try this out with commands like

```
PRINT WORDSORT [FOO BAR CAT SEAL BEAR ZOO]
```

or

```
MAKE "BIRDS [ROBIN CANARY BLUEBIRD SPARROW]
MAKE "BIRDS WORDSORT :BIRDS
PRINT :BIRDS
```

Although it is good to be able to sort words with this new procedure, it would be better to have one procedure that sorts both words and numbers with equal facility. But **LESS.THAN** does not sort numbers well. If it is given two numbers as input, **LESS.THAN** checks the ASCII values of their digits rather than their absolute numeric values. Accordingly, 21 is **LESS.THAN** 22, but 156 is **LESS.THAN** 21, because the leading 1 in 156 has a lower ASCII value than the leading 2 in 21. This procedure hence fails to display Logo's usual ability to work equally well with both numeric and textual data. Many Logo primitives work well whether they get numbers or words as input, and our extensions should do the same when possible.

In order to be able to sort words or numbers with the same procedure, we must modify **LESS.THAN** so that it will work for words or numbers. You remember that we used the Logo primitive < to test numbers when they were being inserted into a list, and our procedure **LESS.THAN** to test words. Now we can write a new procedure that combines the abilities of both < and **LESS.THAN**.

This new procedure takes two inputs, either numbers or words, and outputs **TRUE** if the first input is less than or equal to the second:

```
TO LESS.THAN.OR.EQUAL :ITEM1 :ITEM2
IF AND NUMBERP :ITEM1
      NUMBERP :ITEM2
   [OUTPUT NOT :ITEM1 > :ITEM2]
   [OUTPUT LESS.THAN :ITEM1 :ITEM2]
END
```

LESS.THAN.OR.EQUAL uses the Logo primitive > if both inputs are numbers. Otherwise, it uses the previously defined **LESS.THAN** to compare the inputs. If one of the inputs is a number and the other is not, then the number is tested as if it were a word—by the ASCII values of its digits rather than its numeric value.

To incorporate this new capability into the sorting procedures, just substitute **LESS.THAN.OR.EQUAL** in place of < or **LESS.THAN** in **INSERT** or **INSERT.WORD**. Because the rest of each procedure relies on Logo primitives that work equally well with numbers or words, nothing else needs to be changed. Once modified in this way, these sorting procedures can sort lists such as **[A F 23 T 55 B]**. This illustrates one major difference between Logo and other computer languages such as Pascal that make strong distinctions between numeric and textual data.

Taking this discussion one step further, you can design procedures that also sort lists that contain sublists, such as **[[D A X] Z 29]**. To do this you first define a set of rules that determine under what circumstances one list is to be considered less than another list. Once these rules are made, then they can be translated into a Logo procedure and applied to the general sorting algorithm that we have developed here.

MERGE.SORT

Merge sorting is more subtle than insert sorting. **MERGE.SORT** repeatedly breaks a list of numbers into smaller parts, sorts the parts, and then merges the sorted parts back together.

We can break a list into two parts by putting the odd (first, third, fifth, and so on) members and the even members into separate lists. To get the odds and evens, we can define a pair of procedures that use each other in a clever way:

```
TO ODDS :LIST
IF EMPTYP :LIST
    [OUTPUT []]
OUTPUT FPUT FIRST :LIST
               EVENS BUTFIRST :LIST
END


TO EVENS :LIST
IF EMPTYP :LIST
    [OUTPUT []]
OUTPUT ODDS BUTFIRST :LIST
END
```

These procedures take advantage of the fact that the even members of a list are the same as the odd members of the **BUTFIRST** of that list. Play with them awhile until you see the simplicity of the approach. Try commands like

```
PRINT ODDS [FOO BAR BAT GAR]
PRINT EVENS [2 5 1 4 8 9]
```

Now that we have a tool to break a list into smaller parts, we can define how those small lists can be merged. Actually, the lists that we merge must themselves be sorted already, but you will see that breaking the lists into smaller and smaller pieces until the pieces have only one member each makes this restriction unimportant. This is because when two one-member lists are merged, they are already sorted, and the product of their merger is thus sorted.

With this in mind, we can define a procedure to merge to already sorted lists:

```
TO MERGE :LIST1 :LIST2
IF EMPTYP :LIST1
    [OUTPUT :LIST2]
IF EMPTYP :LIST2
    [OUTPUT :LIST1]
IF FIRST :LIST1 < FIRST :LIST2
    [OUTPUT FPUT FIRST :LIST1
              MERGE BUTFIRST :LIST1
                    :LIST2
     ]
    ; ELSE
    [OUTPUT FPUT FIRST :LIST2
              MERGE :LIST1
                    BUTFIRST :LIST2
     ]
END
```

As **MERGE** goes through the lists, it always picks the smaller of the first elements in **:LIST1** and **:LIST2** and places that element in line for the final output with **FPUT**. This is similar to the accumulation technique that we have used throughout this chapter. Since the lists are already sorted before they are given to **MERGE**, there is no chance that a larger element will be found out of order in either of the two lists, so the task of merging boils down to selecting the smaller first element each time through. This continues until one of the lists is empty, at which point the remainder of the other list, whose elements must all be greater than or equal to any yet encountered, is output along with the waiting queue of selected elements. Experiment with this procedure to see how it works:

```
PRINT MERGE [3] [2]
PRINT MERGE [2 6 9] [3 4 7]
PRINT MERGE [10 20 30] [25 26 27]
```

Note that **MERGE** doesn't work if the lists aren't already sorted:

```
PRINT MERGE [3 5 2] [7 9 4]
```

Figure 4.4 shows how the elements of the two lists are picked off one by one and put in line for eventual accumulation into the last output list.

Finally, with tools to split the list into smaller parts and merge the parts, we can define the procedure that performs the **MERGE.SORT**:

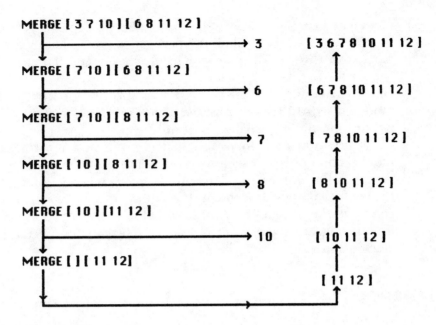

Figure 4.4
MERGE

```
TO MERGE.SORT :LIST
IF EMPTYP :LIST
      [OUTPUT []]    ; SAFETY CHECK
IF EMPTYP BUTFIRST :LIST
      [OUTPUT :LIST]    ; SINGLE ELEMENT
OUTPUT MERGE MERGE.SORT ODDS :LIST
            MERGE.SORT EVENS :LIST
END
```

You can try this out with commands like

```
PRINT MERGE.SORT [3 7 1 12 99 21 33]
```

or

```
MAKE "NUMBERS [3 7 1 12 99 21 33]
MAKE "NUMBERS MERGE.SORT :NUMBERS
PRINT :NUMBERS
```

Figure 4.5 shows how a list of numbers is repeatedly broken down by **EVEN** and **ODD** until all the parts have only one member. Then the parts are **MERGE**d together, one level at a time, until the final sorted list is produced.

You can modify **MERGE.SORT** to sort lists of words, much as we modified **INSORT**. You must use **LESS.THAN** instead of < in **MERGE**, but beyond that the change is not difficult.

The sorting techniques shown here produce sequential lists of either numbers or words, in ascending order. They are convenient for ordering data, but they don't really offer an advantage when it comes to searching the list for a particular element. If you want to sort data items so that they can be retrieved quickly, you should look at the section in chapter 6 on tree sorting. Sorting data into trees can substantially speed the finding of elements in a list.

SUMMARY

None of these sorting tools changes the global value of any object in the workspace. You can thus fit them into various contexts without having to worry about side effects. This allows modular programming. These

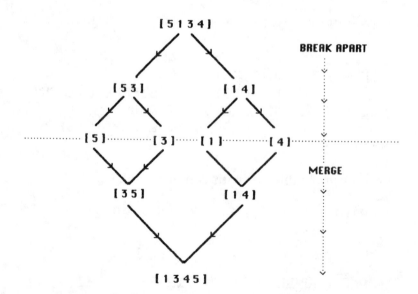

Figure 4.5
MERGE.SORT

tools are not terribly user-friendly. They probably function best when surrounded by a shell of procedures that get the proper inputs and communicate with the user. The flexibility to accept levels of procedures that vary in their friendliness is one of the best features of Logo.

Most of the procedures in this chapter use **FPUT** to accumulate output in a queue, awaiting the ultimate output of the recursive chain. The process resembles the working of a mine-shaft elevator: the first one off is the last one picked up. Recursion and **FPUT** can be similarly combined to solve many kinds of problems.

These procedures make heavy use of recursion to accomplish their goals. The techniques outlined here will be applied often in the rest of the projects in this book. Although many of the tasks to be discussed can be performed without recursion, the use of recursion generally leads to elegant, if somewhat dense, solutions. One of the attractions of programming in Logo is the ease with which these elegant solutions can be defined and implemented.

5 PROPERTY LISTS

THE FUNDAMENTALS ————————————————

Most versions of Logo can create and maintain *property lists*. Property lists allow any Logo word to be linked to one or more *properties*, and these properties can then be given *values*. The value of the word itself is independent of the value of its properties (Appendix A). Thus, a word "**CLASS.LIST** can have the value **[BILL SUE EVELYN]**. Its properties can include "**SUBJECT**, "**MEETING.PLACE**, and "**MEETING.TIME**. If we change the value of "**CLASS.LIST** to **[BILL SUE EVELYN FRED]**, the value of the "**MEETING.TIME** property is unaffected. Properties are listed in the following format:

```
WORD'S PROPERTY IS VALUE
```

In our example, the properties might look like this:

```
CLASS.LIST'S SUBJECT IS [ART HISTORY]
CLASS.LIST'S MEETING.PLACE IS FORUM
CLASS.LIST'S MEETING.TIME IS [MWF 3:00]
```

The value of a property, like the value of any Logo object, can be a word, a number, or a list. In fact, property lists started out in earlier systems as regular lists with three members: the word, the property, and the value. As three-member lists, our example properties would look like this:

```
[CLASS.LIST SUBJECT [ART HISTORY]]
[CLASS.LIST MEETING.PLACE FORUM]
[CLASS.LIST MEETING.TIME [MWF 3:00]]
```

Appendix C presents a set of procedures that mimic the action of the property-list primitives discussed in the rest of this chapter. If you are using a version of Logo that does not directly support property lists, enter the procedures listed in Appendix C before proceeding here. Once you have entered the procedures, you can follow all the examples that deal with property lists in this chapter. Even if you are using a version of Logo that supports property lists, you may want to look at the procedures in Appendix C anyway to see how property lists work in general.

To create a property for an object, you use the primitive **PPROP**. **PPROP** takes three inputs: a word, the name of a property, and the value of the property. To define the properties listed above, you enter

```
PPROP "CLASS.LIST "SUBJECT [ART HISTORY]
PPROP "CLASS.LIST "MEETING.PLACE "FORUM
PPROP "CLASS.LIST "MEETING.TIME [MWF 3:00]
```

The format of **PPROP** comes very close to that in which properties are printed out. **PPS** (*print out properties*) is the command you use to see a listing of all the properties that are currently defined in your workspace. You can use it any time you want to see all the properties. If you use it after entering the statements listed above, you see

```
CLASS.LIST'S SUBJECT IS [ART HISTORY]
CLASS.LIST'S MEETING.PLACE IS FORUM
CLASS.LIST'S MEETING.TIME IS [MWF 3:00]
```

If you want to see just one property (say, for instance, the "**MEETING.PLACE** property of "**CLASS.LIST**), then you can use the **GPROP** (*get property*) primitive. **GPROP** needs two inputs: a word and the name of a property. **GPROP** then outputs the current value of the given property of the given word. To see the "**MEETING.PLACE** property of "**CLASS.LIST**, therefore, you can type

```
PRINT GPROP "CLASS.LIST "MEETING.PLACE
```

Notice that in contrast to **PPS**, which always prints out all properties, **GPROP** merely outputs the value of one property. It must consequently be used as input to some other procedure or primitive. This makes **GPROP** much more versatile than **PPS**, for **PPS** can only print properties, but the output from **GPROP** can be used by other Logo procedures as input. Throughout the rest of this chapter we shall exploit the versatility of **GPROP** to examine and modify the data contained in the property lists.

There is a fourth primitive dealing with property lists besides **PPROP**, **GPROP**, and **PPS**. **REMPROP** (*remove property*) takes two inputs, a word and a property name, and removes the named property from the property list of the input word. You can use it to get rid of properties that you do not want in your workspace. **ERALL**, which erases all the procedures and named objects in the workspace, does not erase property lists in Apple Logo and many other versions of Logo. Try **REMPROP** now:

```
REMPROP "CLASS.LIST "SUBJECT
PPS
```

These four primitives allow you to define, examine, modify, and even delete properties from your workspace. In many cases, simply assigning values to words is sufficient to represent the relationships of data. In other examples, two of which we shall explore in this chapter, property lists offer a superior means by which you can establish data structures that are flexible and easy to work with.

BUILDING AN INDEX

Let's say that you want to keep an index of word references as you read through a book. One way of doing it is to make a note card for each word of interest and then write down the page numbers on which that word appears. But as you go through the book, your stack of cards gets bigger, and as you begin to reencounter words, you have to shuffle through the cards to find the proper card on which to note a new page number.

How can you get Logo to help you keep track of an index? Your first inclination might be to write a short procedure that asks you for the word and page number(s) and then assigns the number(s) as the value of the word. If a word is encountered more than once, its subsequent page numbers can be added to the original list of numbers assigned to the word. The procedure might look something like this:

```
TO INDEX
TYPE [WORD>>>]
MAKE "WORD FIRST READLIST
TYPE [PAGES>>>]
MAKE "PAGES READLIST
; HAS THE WORD BEEN SEEN BEFORE?
IF NOT NAMEP :WORD
     ; DEFINE IT NOW
     [MAKE :WORD []]
; ADD PAGE NUMBERS TO PREVIOUS LIST
MAKE :WORD SENTENCE :PAGES THING :WORD
; GO BACK FOR MORE
INDEX
END
```

You can see that this is actually fairly involved. First, the word and the page numbers have to be assigned to temporary variables. Then the procedure uses **IF NOT NAMEP :WORD** to see if the current word has had a value assigned to it before, because if it hasn't, then trying to add to its value in the next step results in an error. Finally, the page numbers contained in **:PAGES** are joined with the other page numbers (which may be **[ ]** if this is the first time through for the word) contained in **THING :WORD**.

A sample run will clarify this. Suppose we are entering the word **"DOGFOOD** and the page numbers **[10 21 30]**. As the procedure moves on, **NAMEP** checks to see if **"DOGFOOD** has any previous value assigned to it. Let's say here that it has not, so **"DOGFOOD** is given the value **[ ]**. If **"DOGFOOD** had been entered before, then its value would be a list of one or more page numbers. In either case, the value of **"DOGFOOD**, retrieved by **THING :WORD** (**:WORD** evaluating as **"DOGFOOD**), is combined with the value of **"PAGES**, and that is used as the new value of **"DOGFOOD**.

Although this is not the most elegant Logo procedure ever written, it works. It does, however, have one serious weakness. If you try to enter the word **"WORD** and then some pages, the value of **"WORD**, which should be holding the list of page numbers, is wiped out the next time the procedure cycles through and accepts input. Also, you cannot use the word **"PAGES** because its value is also changed every cycle. Of course, you can just choose unlikely names such as **"WORD.1** or **"PAGE.1** for these variables and thus avoid any conflict, but that solution, although workable, seems inelegant.

There is another strategy, however, for solving the index problem. We can introduce the use of property lists to get rid of the bug we discussed above. In our new procedure, each word that we encounter is assigned a **"PAGE.NUMBERS** property. You will see that properties are easier to update than word values and, in addition, have fewer side effects in the workspace:

```
TO INDEX
TYPE [WORD>>>]
MAKE "WORD FIRST READLIST
TYPE [PAGES>>>]
MAKE "PAGES READLIST
PPROP :WORD
      "PAGE.NUMBERS
      SENTENCE :PAGES
             GPROP :WORD "PAGE.NUMBERS
; GO BACK FOR MORE
INDEX
END
```

Notice that the procedure does not have to check to see if the word that is typed in has been encountered before. If the word has been used before, then **GPROP :WORD "PAGE.NUMBERS** gets the old value of the **"PAGE.NUMBERS** property. If no page numbers have been assigned to that property before, then **GPROP** simply returns the empty list (**[ ]**). In the first index procedure, which does not use property lists, we had to do this kind of thing explicitly; here it is done automatically. This is one of the advantages of using property lists over using regular lists.

In this procedure, **PPROP** takes the word that is input and gives it a **"PAGE.NUMBERS** property that is a combination of the current page numbers just entered and the previous page numbers entered (which may be **[ ]**). These two are combined by the step

```
SENTENCE :PAGES
         GPROP :WORD "PAGE.NUMBERS
```

Using this method of keeping track of the pages, you can enter any word, including **"WORD** and **"PAGES**. The subsequent values assigned to **"WORD** and **"PAGES**, which caused a bug in the first version, have no effect on the value of the **"PAGE.NUMBERS** property of either **"WORD** or **"PAGE**.

This procedure illustrates two advantages of property lists: they do not have to be declared before they are used, and they are relatively immune from side effects of other processes in the Logo workspace. It also illustrates how **PPROP** and **GPROP** can be used together, with the output of **GPROP** fetching information that is used as input into **PPROP**. We shall rely on this relationship greatly in the next project.

THE BLOCKS WORLD ───────────────────

One of the most famous environments developed by researchers in artificial intelligence is the *blocks world*, in which the computer knows about a set of blocks and can move them around the screen. The system is smart enough to know that if it wants to move a block that is under another block, it must first move the top block and then move the bottom block. The blocks world has been used to explore many topics in artificial intelligence, including the computer's ability to take natural-language input and the computer's ability to use digital vision.

With Logo we can create a simple blocks microworld in which the computer knows about certain objects and can move them around intelligently. To do this we need to use property lists. This project will let you see how property lists can be used to guide a program's execution and how the program can modify the property lists as it goes along.

Imagine a microworld in which there are four objects: a square block, a rectangular block, a triangular block, and a ball. We can represent the relationships between these objects by assigning properties to the various objects. For instance, if the square is on top of the rectangle, we can say that the square's "**SITS.ON** property is "**RECTANGLE**. We can also say that the rectangle's "**SITS.UNDER** property is "**SQUARE**. If an object is not sitting on any other object, we can say that its "**SITS.ON** property is [ ]. In the same way, an object that does not have anything sitting on it has a "**SITS.UNDER** property of [ ]. This way the computer can keep track of how objects are related. For the version that we are going to develop here, we shall be concerned only with whether objects are sitting on or under other objects. It would not take a great deal of effort, however, to incorporate other properties such as "**NEXT.TO**.

Setting Up the Blocks

First, we must create a set of relationships for the four objects in this microworld. Put the square on top of the rectangle:

```
PPROP "SQUARE "SITS.ON "RECTANGLE
PPROP "RECTANGLE "SITS.UNDER "SQUARE
```

Now put the ball on top of the triangle (ignoring for the moment that this is physically very difficult):

```
PPROP "BALL "SITS.ON "TRIANGLE
PPROP "TRIANGLE "SITS.UNDER "BALL
```

Also make it clear that the ball and the square are on the tops of the stacks—that is, they don't sit under anything:

```
PPROP "BALL "SITS.UNDER []
PPROP "SQUARE "SITS.UNDER []
```

And, finally, establish that the rectangle and the triangle are on the bottoms of the stacks—that is, they don't sit on anything:

```
PPROP "RECTANGLE "SITS.ON []
PPROP "TRIANGLE "SITS.ON []
```

Now type **PPS** to print the properties that are in your workspace so far. You should see the following:

```
TRIANGLE'S SITS.ON IS []
TRIANGLE'S SITS.UNDER IS BALL
SQUARE'S SITS.UNDER IS []
SQUARE'S SITS.ON IS RECTANGLE
RECTANGLE'S SITS.ON IS []
RECTANGLE'S SITS.UNDER IS SQUARE
BALL'S SITS.UNDER IS []
BALL'S SITS.ON IS TRIANGLE
```

These data govern the execution of the program. This is the most fundamental level of representation that we shall use to define the relationships between the objects. At this point we need some procedures that can look at the properties and draw conclusions about the relationships of the objects.

Manipulating the Blocks

First, define a procedure that takes an object name as an input and outputs "**TRUE** if that object is the top one in a stack. If an object is at the top of a stack in the blocks world, its "**SITS.UNDER** property is **[ ]**. Knowing this, you can write this procedure:

```
TO TOP? :OBJECT
IF EQUALP (GPROP :OBJECT "SITS.UNDER) []
     [OP "TRUE]
     [OP "FALSE]
END
```

This procedure looks up the "**SITS.UNDER** property of the input object with the **GPROP** primitive. If the property is equal to **[ ]**, then the procedure outputs "**TRUE**; otherwise it outputs "**FALSE**. Of course, this procedure can also be written in a more condensed fashion, with the result of the **EQUALP** statement output directly:

```
TO TOP? :OBJECT
OP EQUALP (GPROP :OBJECT "SITS.UNDER) []
END
```

There is no functional difference between these two versions of **TOP?** and which one you choose is mostly a matter of style. Generally, any procedure that tests for a condition and then outputs "**TRUE** or "**FALSE** can be written in the condensed form.

The primitive **GPROP** (*get property*) is used to look up a particular property of a specific object. It takes two inputs: the name of an object and the name of a property. It returns the value of the named property. Here it is used to find the "**SITS.UNDER** property of the object given to **TOP?** as input. If **GPROP** tries to look up a property that does not exist at the time, it returns **[ ]**. There is no error message, as there is if we try to get the value of a variable that has not been defined.

Now that we can determine if any object is on the top of a stack, we can also define a similar procedure to find out if an object is on the bottom of a stack. An object is on the bottom when its "**SITS.ON** property is **[ ]**.

```
TO BOTTOM? :OBJECT
OP EQUALP (GPROP :OBJECT "SITS.ON) []
END
```

Now try out these two procedures in the blocks world we defined earlier. Remember that the ball is sitting on the triangle and the square is sitting on the rectangle. If you typed in the properties in the first part of this section, you can use **TOP?** and **BOTTOM?** now to examine the state of the blocks world. Try these:

```
PRINT TOP? "SQUARE          true
PRINT BOTTOM? "BALL         false
PRINT TOP? "BALL            true
PRINT BOTTOM? "SQUARE       false
```

Try some other combinations for yourself and see whether **TOP?** and **BOTTOM?** always give the correct answers.

Next, let's take the square off the rectangle. To do this we must use **PPROP** to define the new state of the world:

```
PPROP "SQUARE "SITS.ON []
PPROP "RECTANGLE "SITS.UNDER []
```

Now the square does not sit on anything, and the rectangle does not sit on anything. At this point **PPS** looks something like this:

```
TRIANGLE'S SITS.ON IS []
TRIANGLE'S SITS.UNDER IS BALL
SQUARE'S SITS.UNDER IS []
SQUARE'S SITS.ON IS []
RECTANGLE'S SITS.ON IS []
RECTANGLE'S SITS.UNDER IS []
BALL'S SITS.UNDER IS []
BALL'S SITS.ON IS TRIANGLE
```

The square and the rectangle are sitting by themselves, while the ball is sitting on top of the triangle. Now try our procedures again:

```
PRINT TOP? "SQUARE          true
PRINT BOTTOM? "SQUARE       true
PRINT TOP? "RECTANGLE       true
PRINT BOTTOM? "RECTANGLE    true
PRINT TOP? "TRIANGLE        false
PRINT BOTTOM? "TRIANGLE     true
PRINT TOP? "BALL            true
PRINT BOTTOM? "BALL         false
```

You can see from this that if an object is sitting all by itself, it is at both the top and the bottom of a stack of one object.

It is awkward to have to use **PPROP** directly to change the relationships of the objects in the blocks world; we need to develop some procedures to change them for us. We can write a layer of procedures around the nuts-and-bolts manipulations done by **PPROP** and **GPROP**. Indeed, very often Logo programming involves adding ever-expanding shells of procedures that tend to make the inner workings of the system invisible to the user. Just as we don't have to worry about the actual machine instructions that are executed when we use **PPROP**, so we won't have to worry even about **PPROP** once the next layer is written. We are creating a specialized extension to Logo that is tailored to the problems in the blocks world.

First, imagine a procedure that takes one object as an input and then updates the properties so that if the object is sitting on top of another object, it is taken off and put by itself on the floor. The procedure first checks to see if the input object is in fact sitting on top of another object. If it isn't, then there is no need to proceed. If the input object is sitting on top of another object, then the procedure has to see if the input object is sitting under any other object, and if so, move the top object first before moving the input object. The procedure also must make sure that the "**SITS.UNDER** property of the object on the bottom is changed after the top object is moved.

Let's walk through an example. Right now, the ball is still on top of the triangle. If we want to move the ball but aren't sure of its position, we must first check to see if the ball is already at the bottom of the stack— to see if **BOTTOM?** "**BALL** returns the value "**TRUE**. In this case, the ball is not the bottom object of a stack, so we see if there is any object on top of the ball. We can do this with **TOP?** "**BALL**. Since the ball is the top object we can move it. If there were an object on top of the ball, we would have to move that object first and then move the ball.

Because the triangle is under the ball, we must first change the **SITS.UNDER** property of the triangle to **[ ]**. To find out which object is under the ball, we can use **GPROP** "**BALL** "**SITS.ON**. This gives us the name of the object on which the ball is sitting. We can then use that name to update the property of the object that was underneath the ball. In this particular case we have to change the **SITS.UNDER** property of **GPROP** "**BALL** "**SITS.ON**, which is "**TRIANGLE**, to **[ ]**. We needed to use the **SITS.ON** property of the ball to find out which object was below it, so we did not change that property until we had first changed the **SITS.UNDER** property of the triangle. Now we can change the **SITS.ON** property of the ball. It no longer sits on the triangle, so we change its **SITS.ON** property to **[ ]**.

Now, let's write a procedure. The object we input to this procedure is moved so that it is by itself. If it is under other objects, they are moved first by the same procedure, and then the original object is moved. Any object that is under an object that is moved must have its properties changed to reflect the fact that it is no longer under the moved object:

```
TO PUT.DOWN :OBJECT
IF BOTTOM? :OBJECT
      ; QUIT WHILE YOU'RE AHEAD
      [STOP]
IF NOT TOP? :OBJECT
      ; MOVE NEXT OBJECT UP STACK
      [PUT.DOWN (GPROP :OBJECT "SITS.UNDER)]
; CHANGE PROPERTY OF OBJECT UNDERNEATH
PPROP (GPROP :OBJECT "SITS.ON)
      "SITS.UNDER
      []
; CHANGE THE PROPERTY OF THE TOP OBJECT
PPROP :OBJECT "SITS.ON []
END
```

If you use this procedure by typing

`PUT.DOWN "BALL`

and then **PPS**, you see that the ball is now all by itself and no longer sits on the triangle.

Note that **PUT.DOWN** continues to call itself recursively until all the objects above the original object have been **PUT.DOWN**, and then continues with the task of moving the original. This way, **PUT.DOWN** can get to an object at any level in a stack. This process of recursively moving the upper blocks is shown diagrammatically in figure 5.1. Imagine that the blocks are stacked up with the rectangle on the bottom, then the square, then the ball, and finally the triangle. As you can see, a call to **PUT.DOWN "SQUARE** elicits a call to **PUT.DOWN "BALL**, and then that calls **PUT.DOWN "TRIANGLE**. Remember that the action of a procedure that makes a recursive call is suspended until the action of the recursive call is finished. The last recursive level called is the first one

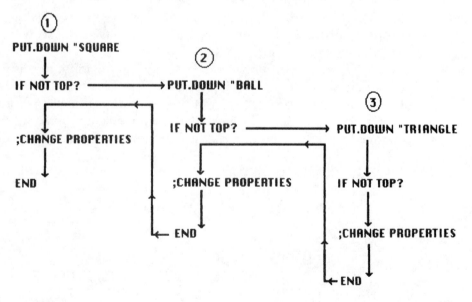

Figure 5.1
PUT.DOWN

finished, then the system backs out of its recursive tunnel and continues with processing the next-to-last procedure called, and so on until the system has worked its way back to the original procedure. In our example, the moving of the square is suspended while the ball is moved, but the moving of the ball is suspended until the triangle is moved. Once the triangle is moved, the moving of the ball can be finished, and after that the moving of the square is completed.

At this point all the objects in the blocks world are sitting by themselves. You have seen how to dismantle stacks of blocks, both by direct manipulation of the properties of the objects involved and also with the **PUT.DOWN** procedure. We now need a procedure that allows us to stack the blocks. This procedure takes two inputs: an object to be moved and an object onto which the first object is to be moved. We can call these two inputs **:ITEM1** and **:ITEM2**; when the procedure is finished, the first object is on top of the second.

The procedure must first check to see if the object that it wishes to move, **:ITEM1**, is on the top of a stack. If it isn't, then the object or objects that are on top of it must be moved first. We can use **PUT.DOWN** to remove the objects above. Also, if the destination object, **:ITEM2**, is not on the top of a stack, then objects above it must also be moved with the **PUT.DOWN** procedure before we can put a new object there. Next, the procedure must check to see if **:ITEM1** is sitting on top of another object, and if it is, the lower object's **SITS.UNDER** property must be changed to reflect the movement of the upper object. Finally, the properties of **:ITEM1** and **:ITEM2** must be changed to reflect the new relationship: **:ITEM1** on top of **:ITEM2**.

Let's walk through an example. Suppose the square is on top of the ball. We want to put the ball on the triangle, which is sitting by itself. First, we see if the ball, which is the object we want to move, is on the top of a stack. In this case it isn't, so we use **PUT.DOWN** to move the square off the ball. Once **PUT.DOWN** has cleared off the top of the ball, we see if the destination, the triangle, is on top of a stack. In this case it is, so we don't need to clear a space for the ball. Now we are ready to move the ball onto the triangle, but first we must make sure that any object under the ball has its properties changed to reflect the ball's departure. Once that is done we can update the properties of the ball and the triangle to show that the ball is now on top of the triangle. There are three main conditions to check, and then the actual move:

```
TO PUT.ON :ITEM1 :ITEM2
IF NOT TOP? :ITEM1
    ; MOVE THE UPPER OBJECTS
    [PUT.DOWN (GPROP :ITEM1 "SITS.UNDER)]
IF NOT TOP? :ITEM2
    ; CLEAR LANDING SPOT
    [PUT.DOWN (GPROP :ITEM2 "SITS.UNDER)]
IF NOT BOTTOM? :ITEM1
    ; CHANGE PROPERTY OF OBJECT UNDERNEATH
    [PPROP (GPROP :ITEM1 "SITS.ON)
        "SITS.UNDER
        []
    ]    ; END PPROP
; CHANGE PROPERTIES OF MAIN OBJECTS
PPROP :ITEM1 "SITS.ON :ITEM2
PPROP :ITEM2 "SITS.UNDER :ITEM1
END
```

Try this procedure now, but be careful because it is not yet smart enough to deal with improper input. It doesn't do well, for instance, if you try to put an object on itself. Moreover, if you try to use objects that are not already in the property lists, you get strange results. Check the current status of the blocks world before you start with **PPS**, and then after each use of **PUT.ON** check again to see that the procedure is working as you expected.

Let's add a few steps to **PUT.ON** to make it sufficiently intelligent to deal with some particular input combinations. As mentioned above, an object cannot be placed on itself. This is easy to check for:

```
IF EQUALP :ITEM1 :ITEM2
    [STOP]
```

Also, the procedure must check to see if **:ITEM1** is already on top of **:ITEM2**, in which case it must stop:

```
TO ALREADY.THERE :ITEM1 :ITEM2
OP EQUALP (GPROP :ITEM1 "SITS.ON) :ITEM2
END
```

We trap these special cases first, before the procedure has a chance to do anything serious with the inputs. Putting these traps into the original **PUT.ON** procedure, we now have

```
TO PUT.ON :ITEM1 :ITEM2
IF EQUALP :ITEM1 :ITEM2
        ; CAN'T PUT ITEM ON ITSELF
        [STOP]
IF ALREADY.THERE :ITEM1 :ITEM2
        ; QUIT WHILE YOU'RE AHEAD
        [STOP]
IF NOT TOP? :ITEM1
        ; MOVE THE UPPER OBJECTS
        [PUT.DOWN (GPROP :ITEM1 "SITS.UNDER)]
IF NOT TOP? :ITEM2
        ; CLEAR A LANDING SPOT
        [PUT.DOWN (GPROP :ITEM2 "SITS.UNDER)]
IF NOT BOTTOM? :ITEM1
        ; CHANGE PROPERTY OF OBJECT UNDERNEATH
        [PPROP GPROP :ITEM1 "SITS.ON
                "SITS.UNDER
                []
        ]    ; END PPROP
; CHANGE PROPERTIES OF MAIN OBJECTS
PPROP :ITEM1 "SITS.ON :ITEM2
PPROP :ITEM2 "SITS.UNDER :ITEM1
END
```

We have the core of a system that can manipulate and keep track of a collection of objects. It is able to update its data base after each change and then use the new data to guide further changes. It is able to react to novel arrangements of its objects with a fairly simple recursive problem-solving strategy. Property lists are ideal for this type of application because they are easy to access and manipulate and they can accurately represent the relationships between objects.

Adding Graphics to the Blocks World

In the previous section, we developed a way to symbolically represent the spatial relationships of objects in the blocks world. If you spent much time working with that system, you must realize that it is awkward to have to read through the whole list of properties each time you want to figure out what effect your change has had on the objects. Think how much better it would be to see a graphic representation of the relationships between the blocks any time those relationships are changed. We can, in fact, develop a set of procedures to graphically represent the symbolic relationships contained in the property lists. This is a great project for Logo because it requires symbolic and graphic capabilities, both of which Logo possesses.

First, let's write procedures to draw the four different objects in our world: the square, the rectangle, the triangle, and the ball. To make other parts of the system easier to write, let's make all the objects roughly the same size by assuming that each is drawn within a box of fixed dimensions. Furthermore, let's place the turtle in the lower left-hand corner of the imaginary box before it draws the figure, and let's have the turtle return there after the figure is drawn. Our four objects can fit side by side across the screen without touching if the imaginary boxes that contain them are 40 units wide. With these restrictions in mind, let's write the following procedures:

```
TO SQUARE
PD
REPEAT 4 [FD 40 RT 90]
PU
END

TO RECTANGLE
LT 90 PU BK 10 RT 90 PD
REPEAT 2 [FD 40 RT 90 FD 20 RT 90]
LT 90 PU FD 10 RT 90
END

TO TRIANGLE
RT 30 PD
REPEAT 3 [FD 40 RT 120]
LT 30 PU
END

TO BALL
LT 90 PU BK 20 PD
REPEAT 36 [FD 3.14 / 36 * 40 RT 10]
PU FD 20 RT 90
END
```

Note that each procedure takes care of its own **PENUP** and **PENDOWN** commands, so the rest of the system does not need to worry about them. These procedures draw faster if you hide the turtle with **HIDETURTLE**.

Now we need a list of the objects in the blocks world. This list is actually a list of both the objects and the procedures that draw pictures of the objects. This is another one of Logo's strong points, that a Logo word can be the name of a symbolic object, the name of a procedure, or both. We shall exploit that capability here. Enter the following definition of "**OBJECTS**:

```
MAKE "OBJECTS [SQUARE TRIANGLE BALL RECTANGLE]
```

Now we can write a procedure **DRAW.ALL** that steps through the list of objects and draws them on the screen in their correct relative positions. This procedure takes the first element of the list and checks to see if it is at the bottom of any stack. If it isn't the bottom of a stack, then the procedure calls itself recursively with the rest of the list of objects. If the first element of the list is on the bottom of a stack, then the object is handed over to the procedure **DRAW.STACK** and is drawn at the bottom of the screen.

DRAW.STACK then checks to see if there is an object sitting on top of the object it has just drawn. If there is, then the turtle is moved up 40 units, and **DRAW.STACK** is called and draws the next object in the stack. Once again **DRAW.STACK** checks to see if there is an object on top of the object it has just drawn, and if there is it calls itself again with the next object up. This goes on until the entire stack is drawn. The stack is seen recursively as a stack of shorter stacks, and each successive level is treated in the same way.

When **DRAW.STACK** finishes drawing a stack, control returns to **DRAW.ALL**, which goes to the next element of the list to see if it is at the bottom of a stack. Every object in the list is either at the bottom of a stack or on top of another object. In either case it eventually gets handed to **DRAW.STACK** and drawn on the screen. If it is at the bottom of a stack, it is drawn at the bottom of the screen. If it is on top of another object, then it is drawn on the upper edge of that object. In this way all the objects are drawn in their correct positions.

For example, suppose that the square is on top of the ball and that the rectangle and the triangle are by themselves. Let's go through our list of objects

```
[SQUARE TRIANGLE BALL RECTANGLE]
```

and do the following. First, with **DRAW.ALL** let's look at the first element of the list. Is the square at the bottom of a stack? Since the answer is no (because it is on top of the ball), we look at the next element of the list. The triangle is the bottom of a stack, so we give it to **DRAW.STACK**, and it is drawn. Since there is no object on top of the triangle, we go back to **DRAW.ALL** and look at the next member of the list. The ball is at the bottom of a stack, so it is drawn by **DRAW.STACK**. Since the square is on top of the ball, it is drawn by **DRAW.STACK** at the upper edge of the ball. There is nothing on top of the square, so we return to **DRAW.ALL** and look at the last member of the list. The rectangle is at the bottom of a stack, so it is drawn at the lower edge of the screen by **DRAW.STACK**. If you followed that, then you are ready to define the two procedures:

```
TO DRAW.ALL :LIST
IF EMPTYP :LIST
     [STOP]
IF BOTTOM? FIRST :LIST
     ; DRAW A STACK
     [DRAW.STACK FIRST :LIST]
; MOVE OVER TO THE RIGHT
RT 90 FD 50 LT 90
; GET THE NEXT OBJECT
DRAW.ALL BUTFIRST :LIST
END

TO DRAW.STACK :OBJECT
; GET PROCEDURE TO DRAW OBJECT
RUN (SENTENCE :OBJECT)
IF NOT TOP? :OBJECT
     ; DRAW THE NEXT OBJECT IN STACK
     [FD 40
      DRAW.STACK (GPROP :OBJECT "SITS.UNDER)
      BK 40
      ]    ; END THEN
END
```

These procedures are much like the procedures that we used to move the objects symbolically. The only new idea is in **DRAW.STACK**: the name of the object is used by **RUN** to execute the procedure of the same name. **RUN** expects its input to be in a list, so the object name is put into a list by **(SENTENCE :OBJECT)**.

Now that we have these graphic procedures, we don't have to check the property list to see if each change is done correctly. We have on the screen a graphic representation of the state of the properties.

To make these new procedures more usable, let's write a shell procedure called **UPDATE** that takes care of the initial turtle position and then calls **DRAW.ALL**:

```
TO UPDATE
CS
PU LT 90 FD 119 LT 90 FD 59 LT 90
PD BK 20 FD 240 BK 240 LT 90 PU
DRAW.ALL :OBJECTS
END
```

UPDATE uses the global value of the list **:OBJECTS** defined earlier.

Now you can try the new system. If all the blocks start out sitting by themselves, the following procedure calls result in screen images like the accompanying figures:

```
UPDATE                              (figure 5.2)
PUT.ON "SQUARE "TRIANGLE
UPDATE                              (figure 5.3)
PUT.ON "BALL "SQUARE
UPDATE                              (figure 5.4)
PUT.DOWN "SQUARE
UPDATE                              (figure 5.5)
```

You can see from the figures that **UPDATE** shows only the final result of any shuffling of the blocks. Intervening moves to get rid of obstacles are not shown. But you can make **UPDATE** a part of the **PUT.DOWN** and **PUT.ON** procedures so that each step of a particular move is shown. Simply put **UPDATE** just before the end statement in **PUT.ON** and **PUT.DOWN**, and the intervening recursive steps that are called to move obstacles are shown, as well as the final state of the blocks. With **UPDATE** added, the two procedures look like this:

Figure 5.2
First UPDATE

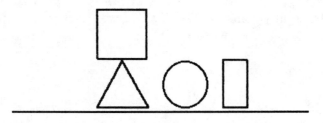

Figure 5.3
UPDATE after PUT.ON "SQUARE "TRIANGLE

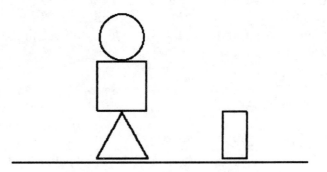

Figure 5.4
UPDATE after PUT.ON "BALL "SQUARE

Figure 5.5
UPDATE after PUT.DOWN "SQUARE

```
TO PUT.ON :ITEM1 :ITEM2
IF EQUALP :ITEM1 :ITEM2
     ; CAN'T PUT OBJECT ON ITSELF
     [STOP]
IF ALREADY.THERE :ITEM1 :ITEM2
     ; QUIT WHILE YOU'RE AHEAD
     [STOP]
IF NOT TOP? :ITEM1
     ; MOVE THE UPPER OBJECTS
     [PUT.DOWN (GPROP :ITEM1 "SITS.UNDER)]
IF NOT TOP? :ITEM2
     ; CLEAR A LANDING SPOT
     [PUT.DOWN (GPROP :ITEM2 "SITS.UNDER)]
IF NOT BOTTOM? :ITEM1
     ; CHANGE PROPERTY OF OBJECT UNDERNEATH
     [PPROP (GPROP :ITEM1 "SITS.ON)
            "SITS.UNDER
            []
     ]    ; END PPROP
; CHANGE PROPERTIES OF MAIN OBJECTS
PPROP :ITEM1 "SITS.ON :ITEM2
PPROP :ITEM2 "SITS.UNDER :ITEM1
; SHOW CHANGES
UPDATE
END


TO PUT.DOWN :OBJECT
IF BOTTOM? :OBJECT
     ; QUIT WHILE YOU'RE AHEAD
     [STOP]
IF NOT TOP? :OBJECT
     ; MOVE NEXT OBJECT UP STACK
     [PUT.DOWN (GPROP :OBJECT "SITS.UNDER)]
; CHANGE PROPERTY OF OBJECT UNDERNEATH
PPROP (GPROP :OBJECT "SITS.ON)
     "SITS.UNDER
     []
; CHANGE THE PROPERTY OF THE TOP OBJECT
PPROP :OBJECT "SITS.ON []
; SHOW CHANGES
UPDATE
END
```

Finally, a short procedure that asks for user input, moves blocks accordingly, and then loops to the beginning is useful. We can call this top-level shell **BLOCKS**. It assumes that all manipulations are of the **PUT.ON** variety (that is, putting one object on a destination object) but recognizes that a destination of "**FLOOR** means that the change is a **PUT.DOWN**. With **BLOCKS** at work, the user is far removed from the nitty-gritty of property lists and can deal with the blocks world on a more familiar, conceptual level:

```
TO BLOCKS
TYPE [OBJECT TO MOVE>>>]
MAKE "ITEM1 FIRST READLIST
TYPE [DESTINATION>>>]
MAKE "ITEM2 FIRST READLIST
IF EQUALP :ITEM2 "FLOOR
     [PUT.DOWN :ITEM1]
     [PUT.ON :ITEM1 :ITEM2]
BLOCKS
END
```

SUMMARY

We have developed a way to symbolically represent the relationships between objects by using property lists. This representation directs the action of the procedures that manipulate the objects and can also direct the action of the procedures that translate the symbolic relationships of the property lists into understandable visual forms. The system we have created here is very simple, but it illustrates one strategy for mimicking intelligence. You can see that developing systems that deal with complex situations intelligently is an enormous task, yet this relatively simple technique could be used as part of a computer program to control industrial robots.

We could extend our blocks procedures by using more objects or by creating more complex relationships between them. For example, without much effort we could make our program smart enough to know that objects really cannot sit on top of other objects that do not have flat tops—balls and triangles, for instance. We could do this simply by having the **PUT.ON** procedure check some sort of **FLAT.TOP** property of any destination object.

You might want to try having more objects than can fit side by side across the screen. That way, at least one object would always have to be sitting on another one. The shortage of floor space would dictate that the procedure look for an open space for any object being moved rather than just set it down.

Another extension, which would be quite involved, would be to attach a limited natural-language *parser* to the system so that the user could type in sentences like Put the square on the triangle, Take the ball off the rectangle, and What is on top of the ball?

Of course, there are many other uses for property lists, particularly in data-base applications. Imagine a data base in which data are represented by properties such as **HYDROGEN'S ATOMIC NUMBER IS 1** or **RECORD#203'S ADDRESS IS 123 FIRST ST.** The concepts discussed here should allow you to use property lists effectively for your own interesting projects.

6 TREES

DRAWING TREES ——————————————————

This chapter is about binary trees, one of which is depicted in figure 6.1. We shall begin by drawing trees, go on to use the tree form to represent the organization of knowledge in expert systems, and finally develop methods that sort data into trees and search for data thus arranged.

The tree in figure 6.1 consists of a straight line rising up and then branching into two straight lines, each of which branches into two straight lines, each of which branches into two straight lines. A tree is made up of smaller trees that are made up of smaller trees . . . and surely a procedure to construct such a tree is a likely application for recursion.

When you are writing a recursive procedure, it is always good strategy to reduce the problem to its simplest case. The most stripped down tree you can draw is simply a staight line with no branches (figure 6.2). We can call this a *level 1* tree. (Chapter 2 on recursive drawing introduced the concept of *level* in recursive procedures. You might want to look at that chapter now if you haven't already done so.) A level 2 tree is a straight trunk with a right branch and a left branch that are each smaller level 1 trees (figure 6.3). A level 3 tree continues this recursive pattern by being a single trunk with right and left branches that are smaller level 2 trees (and you already know what level 2 trees are), as shown in figure 6.4.

Translating this description of trees into a Logo procedure is relatively simple. We can use two inputs, the size of the tree and a level indicator. Any tree of a particular level is made up of a straight line, at one end of which are two trees of the next lowest level. We need to indicate turns to orient the branches properly, and we need to check the level so

Figure 6.1
A binary tree

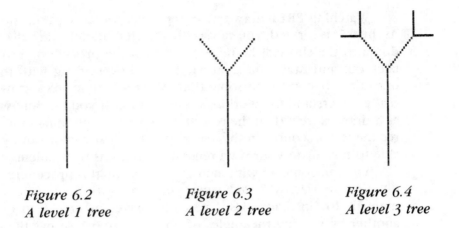

Figure 6.2
A level 1 tree

Figure 6.3
A level 2 tree

Figure 6.4
A level 3 tree

that the procedure stops when it gets down to level 0. We can also put in a peephole to print out the value of each input at each level of the recursion. Thus, as the tree procedure works its way down recursively, the local values of **:SIZE** and **:LEVEL** are printed on the screen, the procedure pauses briefly, and then it continues drawing the tree:

```
TO TREE :SIZE :LEVEL
(PRINT [SIZE =] :SIZE [LEVEL =] :LEVEL)
WAIT 120
IF :LEVEL = 0 [STOP]
FD :SIZE
LT 45
TREE :SIZE / 2 :LEVEL - 1
RT 90
TREE :SIZE / 2 :LEVEL - 1
LT 45
BK :SIZE
END
```

Note that the size is reduced each time the level is reduced. See also how the last step of the procedure returns the turtle to its original position. It is very important that each level of the recursion, after taking the turtle and drawing with it, then return the turtle to where the procedure found it. This way the action of any one level is completely transparent to the rest of the levels. Note also that the sum of right and left turns is a net turn of 0 degrees, so the turtle's heading is also restored by each call to **TREE**.

Watching **TREE** draw trees is a perfect way to see recursion at work. As the tree is formed, you can see that the left branches are all drawn first, down to the shortest branches, and then the procedural levels start to back out and draw the right-hand branches, starting with the smallest ones first. If you spend some time watching these trees grow, you will really understand the workings of recursion. If you can follow the turtle as it draws a tree, then the rest of this chapter, and in fact the rest of the recursive procedures in this book, will be clear to you, and you will be able to formulate your own recursive solutions to problems.

You can come up with many variations on this procedure. Instead of dividing the size by 2 each time, you can multiply by .6 or some other number, for instance. Also, you can make the tree lean one way or another by varying the angles of turn. Figure 6.5 shows the result of a variation of the tree procedure:

```
TO TREE2 :SIZE :LEVEL
(PRINT [SIZE =] :SIZE [LEVEL =] :LEVEL)
IF :LEVEL = 0 [STOP]
FD :SIZE
LT 60
TREE2 :SIZE * .6 :LEVEL - 1
RT 90
TREE2 :SIZE * .7 :LEVEL - 1
LT 30
BK :SIZE
END
```

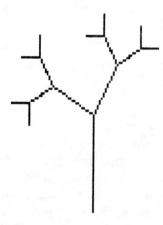

Figure 6.5
TREE2 40 4

TREES AS DATA STRUCTURES

There are many situations in which ideas or objects can be conveniently arranged as trees. These situations generally involve hierarchies, such as that shown in figure 6.6. The mythical company of figure 6.6 is divided into two main divisions, research and production. Research is further divided into two subdivisions, cola and noncola. Production is divided into bottling and canning. The lowest divisions in this diagram could easily be further subdivided. (For our purposes, trees will have only two branches from any node, but procedures can be written for trees with any number of branches.)

TREES AS LISTS

In order to use tree organization in Logo, we must decide how to represent the structure of the tree as a Logo data object. We shall use lists here, although later in the chapter we shall discuss how to use property lists to represent trees. By limiting the branching of our trees to simple binary branching, we can derive a consistent format for representing trees as lists.

The basic repeating structure of a data tree is a node with two branches under it, like a parent with two children. We can represent this as a list of three members. The first member is the parent node, the second member is the left-hand child, and the third member is the right-hand child.

The simplest tree, with just one node and no children, can be represented by the list **[[A] [] []]**. The two empty lists show that there are

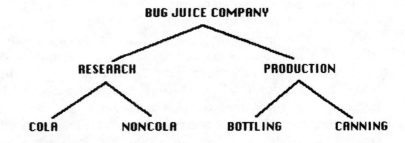

Figure 6.6
A hierarchy

no children of the parent node. The tree shown in figure 6.7 can be represented by the list

[[A] [[B] [] []] [[C] [] []]]

Here you can see that the two children are themselves treated as trees and thus are represented as lists with three members. Going one step further, we can represent the tree shown in figure 6.8 as

[[A] [[B] [[D] [] []] [[E] [] []]] [[C] [[F] []
[]] [[G] [] []]]]

Figure 6.9 shows a tree that is not completely full at all levels. It can be represented as

[[A] [[B] [] [[E] [] []]] [[C] [[D] [] []] []]]

If you try to go any deeper into trees than this, you can get pretty confused representing them in lists, even though the structure is completely consistent. The main thing to remember is that every node is treated as a complete tree and is shown as a three-member list. These three-member lists are nested further and further to show the growing depth of complexity of the tree as a whole.

No one really wants to spend time translating trees into list structures like these, as the activity tends to lead to pulled hair and chewed pencils. Because of its repetitive and consistent nature, this task invites a recursive procedure.

Because the method by which a list represents a tree is so simple and consistent, you can expect the procedure that builds such lists to be short and elegant. When you are struggling to convert an idea into a procedure, simplicity is often the key to success. The procedure that we define to construct tree lists takes a beginning node as input and then outputs a list of that node and the left and right children. Because the children themselves are nodes, they too must be fed back into the procedure so that their children can be added to the final list. This procedure uses what is called a *depth-first* strategy, much as does the procedure that draws trees. It continues to add to the left branch of a tree until it encounters the empty list that signals the end of a branch, at which point it begins to fill in the lowest levels of the right branch and work its way back to the parent node. This procedure uses two subprocedures called **GET.LEFT**

Figure 6.7
A two-level tree

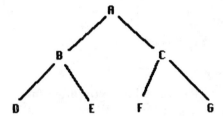

Figure 6.8
A three-level tree

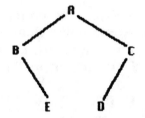

Figure 6.9
An incomplete three-level tree

and **GET.RIGHT** to communicate the current location in the tree and prompt the user for the next element of the tree:

```
TO TREE.BUILDER :NODE
IF EMPTYP :NODE
     [OUTPUT []]
OUTPUT (LIST :NODE
              TREE.BUILDER GET.LEFT :NODE
              TREE.BUILDER GET.RIGHT :NODE
          )
END
```

```
TO GET.LEFT :NODE
PRINT :NODE
PRINT [LEFT BRANCH...?]
OUTPUT READLIST
END

TO GET.RIGHT :NODE
PRINT :NODE
PRINT [RIGHT BRANCH...?]
OUTPUT READLIST
END
```

To use this procedure, you must first have an idea of the structure of your tree. For instance, if the structure is that shown in figure 6.8, you type in

```
PRINT TREE.BUILDER [A]
```

and then answer successive prompts for the left and right branches. When you reach the end of a childless branch, just press the <return> key without typing any letters. This then feeds the empty list to **TREE.BUILDER** and tells it to start back up the tree. Note that the procedure does not set any global values, so if you want to see its product you use it with **PRINT** or **MAKE**.

Work with this tool on a variety of trees until you feel comfortable with it. Doing so is analogous to watching a turtle draw trees, and it helps you understand recursion intuitively. The size of the trees that you build with this tool is arbitrary, within the limits of your computer's memory capacity. If you tackle really big trees, you will appreciate the convenience of this tool over that of putting together the lists by hand. Once again you can construct a Logo procedure that allows you to concentrate on the more familiar aspects of a problem (here, designations for the right and left branches) while the procedure takes care of the details that matter to the computer.

EXPERT SYSTEMS

Up to this point, our trees have been fairly abstract, but data trees can be quite concrete. Imagine that a light goes out in your house and that you phone an electrician. When you converse, the electrician asks you a series of questions in order to discover why the light is not working. Your yes or no answer to each question determines what the electrician says next (figure 6.10).

This (or any other) inquiry that branches in a binary fashion we can represent as a list in Logo, by the method shown in the previous section. Then we can write procedures to take the user through the tree, procedures that branch at each node according to the user's response. In this way we can create an *expert system* whose knowledge is contained in a tree, each node of which is a question, a disclaimer, or a directive for action. To simplify our task, we restrict the questions to the yes-or-no sort. Each childless node is usually a directive to perform some remedial action, or it can be a disclaimer. You can see in figure 6.10 that the expert doesn't know what to do if there is current at the wall, the bulb is good, and the lamp is good. (Surely a real electrician would be similarly stumped in the same circumstances.)

The tools that we need in order to construct expert systems are similar to the ones developed in the previous section. We can modify **GET.LEFT** and **GET.RIGHT** to become **GET.YES** and **GET.NO**. We can use a modified **TREE.BUILDER** that incorporates **GET.YES** and **GET.NO**. One additional procedure, **EXPERT.CONSTRUCTOR**, facilitates the conceptual realization of expert systems. This procedure takes the name of a subject as input and then asks for the first question at the

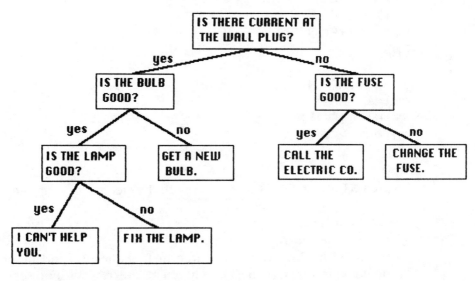

Figure 6.10
An inquiry that branches
in a binary fashion

head of the tree. This first node is then fed directly into the new **TREE.BUILDER2**. When **TREE.BUILDER2** has obtained all the information about the tree and put it into list form, that list is output to the **MAKE** statement, which defines a global variable whose name is the subject and whose value is the tree list. This makes the tree available to other procedures in the workspace and allows it to be saved on disk:

```
TO EXPERT.CONSTRUCTOR :SUBJECT
PRINT [WHAT IS THE FIRST QUESTION?]
MAKE :SUBJECT TREE.BUILDER2 READLIST
END


TO TREE.BUILDER2 :NODE
IF EMPTYP :NODE
     [OUTPUT []]
OUTPUT (LIST :NODE
              TREE.BUILDER2 GET.YES :NODE
              TREE.BUILDER2 GET.NO :NODE
         )
END


TO GET.YES :NODE
PRINT :NODE
PRINT [IF YES...]
OUTPUT READLIST
END


TO GET.NO :NODE
PRINT :NODE
PRINT [IF NO...]
OUTPUT READLIST
END
```

To use **EXPERT.CONSTRUCTOR** with the electricity example, you type

```
EXPERT.CONSTRUCTOR "ELECTRICITY
```

and then follow the prompts to enter the first question and all subsequent branching questions. As before, enter a <return> with no text to signal the end of a childless branch. Figure 6.11 shows a sample interaction between a user and **EXPERT.CONSTRUCTOR**.

```
EXPERT.CONSTRUCTOR "ELECTRICITY
       WHAT IS THE FIRST QUESTION?
IS THERE CURRENT AT THE WALL PLUG?
       IS THERE CURRENT AT THE WALL PLUG?
       IF YES...
IS THE BULB GOOD?
       IS THE BULB GOOD?
       IF YES...
IS THE LAMP GOOD?
       IS THE LAMP GOOD?
       IF YES...
I CAN'T HELP YOU.
       I CAN'T HELP YOU.
       IF YES...
<return>
       I CAN'T HELP YOU.
       IF NO...
<return>
       IS THE LAMP GOOD?
       IF NO...
FIX THE LAMP.
       FIX THE LAMP.
       IF YES...
<return>
       FIX THE LAMP.
       IF NO...
<return>
       IS THE BULB GOOD?
       IF NO...
GET A NEW BULB.
       GET A NEW BULB.
       IF YES...
<return>
       GET A NEW BULB.
       IF NO...
<return>
       IS THERE CURRENT AT THE WALL PLUG?
       IF NO...
IS THE FUSE GOOD?
       IS THE FUSE GOOD?
       IF YES...
CALL THE ELECTRIC CO.
       CALL THE ELECTRIC CO.
       IF YES...
<return>
       CALL THE ELECTRIC CO.
       IF NO...
<return>
       IS THE FUSE GOOD?
       IF NO...
CHANGE THE FUSE.
       CHANGE THE FUSE.
       IF YES...
<return>
       CHANGE THE FUSE.
       IF NO...
<return>
```

Figure 6.11
Interaction with
EXPERT.CONSTRUCTOR

This procedure allows you to create an expert system on almost any subject that can be investigated with yes-or-no questions. It requires you to sketch the tree structure beforehand so that you can respond to the **IF YES** and **IF NO** prompts, but otherwise it takes care of the details of the list structure.

EXPLORING TREES

Now that we can create expert trees, we need some way to get at the information contained in their lists. Because the user of such a system might know nothing about Logo or computers, we need a procedure that insulates most of the details from the user and shows only those aspects of the process that pertain to the problem that the expert system is trying to explore.

The procedure that we use to look at the trees is structurally similar to the procedure that constructed the trees in the first place. It also uses two subprocedures, **LEFT.BRANCH** and **RIGHT.BRANCH**. Remember that our trees are represented as three-member lists. The parent node is the first member. The left branch is the second (**FIRST BUTFIRST**) member. The right branch is the third (**LAST**) member. As the tree is explored, the topmost node is printed out for the user. If the user answers yes, then the procedure echoes the answer and goes on to explore the left branch of the tree. If the user answers no, then the right branch is explored. This process continues until the line of questioning comes to the end of a childless branch.

EXPLORE also uses a procedure, **END.OF.BRANCH**, to see if the right and left branches are empty, indicating that the current node is the end of a childless branch. **END.OF.BRANCH** uses the logical operator **AND** to check both the right and left branches. On the basis of this description, we can define these procedures:

```
TO EXPLORE :TREE
IF EMPTYP :TREE
     [STOP]
PRINT FIRST :TREE
IF END.OF.BRANCH :TREE
     [STOP]
IF READCHAR = "Y    ; CHECK USER RESPONSE
     [PRINT "Y EXPLORE LEFT.BRANCH :TREE]
     [PRINT "N EXPLORE RIGHT.BRANCH :TREE]
END
```

```
TO LEFT.BRANCH :TREE
OUTPUT FIRST BUTFIRST :TREE
END

TO RIGHT.BRANCH :TREE
OUTPUT LAST :TREE
END

TO END.OF.BRANCH :NODE
OUTPUT AND (EMPTYP LEFT.BRANCH :NODE)
            (EMPTYP RIGHT.BRANCH :NODE)
END
```

If you have entered the electricity example discussed above, then you can now type

```
EXPLORE :ELECTRICITY
```

and get a guided tour of the tree of knowledge. If you use **EXPLORE** and interact with the electricity expert, the exchange is like the exchanges shown in figure 6.12. Notice that when the procedure reaches the end of a branch, it stops, and you must restart the procedure if you wish to try a different course through the tree.

BROWSING IN TREES

EXPLORE allows a user to follow a particular path through a knowledge tree. When the end of a branch is reached, the procedure stops. Now let's write a procedure that allows the user to move through a tree at will by giving the user the ability to back up from any node to a higher-level node and then continue browsing through the tree. This procedure gives the user the opportunity to sample a number of different paths through the tree without having to start over again every time he or she reaches the end of a branch.

We can call this new procedure **BROWSE**. It takes a tree list as input and prints the first node of the tree. Then it allows the user to press specific keys to travel to the left, to the right, or upward in the tree. It uses recursion in the same way as **EXPLORE** does except for one important difference. In **EXPLORE**, when the lowest level of recursion terminates, there is nothing to return to at the higher levels, so the entire series of calls ends. In **BROWSE** there is a final recursive call just before

```
? EXPLORE :ELECTRICITY
    IS THERE CURRENT AT THE WALL PLUG?
  Y
    IS THE BULB GOOD?
  N
    GET A NEW BULB.
? EXPLORE :ELECTRICITY
    IS THERE CURRENT AT THE WALL PLUG?
  Y
    IS THE BULB GOOD?
  Y
    IS THE LAMP GOOD?
  N
    FIX THE LAMP.
? EXPLORE :ELECTRICITY
    IS THERE CURRENT AT THE WALL PLUG?
  N
    IS THE FUSE GOOD?
  N
    CHANGE THE FUSE.
? EXPLORE :ELECTRICITY
    IS THERE CURRENT AT THE WALL PLUG?
  Y
    IS THE BULB GOOD?
  Y
    IS THE LAMP GOOD?
  Y
    I CAN'T HELP YOU.
?
```

Figure 6.12
Interaction with EXPLORE

the **END** statement, so that when one of the recursive calls in the body of the procedure stops, control is returned to the next higher level of **BROWSE** that was in effect before the recursion took place. This procedure is more subtle than **EXPLORE**, so it takes a bit more study:

```
TO BROWSE :TREE
IF EMPTYP :TREE
    [PRINT [END OF BRANCH] STOP]
PRINT FIRST :TREE    ; SHOW CURRENT NODE
MAKE "DIRECTION FILTER [Y N U] READCHAR
IF :DIRECTION = "Y
    [BROWSE LEFT.BRANCH :TREE]
    [IF :DIRECTION = "N
        [BROWSE RIGHT.BRANCH :TREE]
        ; ELSE, MUST BE UP
        [STOP]    ; RETURN TO NEXT HIGHEST NODE
    ]
BROWSE :TREE    ; PICK UP WHERE YOU LEFT OFF
END
```

This procedure uses two subprocedures that we developed earlier in this chapter, **LEFT.BRANCH** and **RIGHT.BRANCH**. It also uses a short procedure called **FILTER** to check user input and accept only characters that have meaning to the chain of control decisions that comes after it. **FILTER** uses the primitive **MEMBERP** to see if the character that is typed in is a member of the list that was given as input. If the character is a member of the list, then it is passed on as output. Otherwise, **FILTER** goes around to get another character from the keyboard until it gets one that is acceptable:

```
TO FILTER :LIST :CHARACTER
IF MEMBERP :CHARACTER :LIST
     [OUTPUT :CHARACTER]
     [OUTPUT FILTER :LIST READCHAR]
END
```

Each level of recursion in **BROWSE** keeps its own copy of the portion of the tree that it is looking at. This is why the appropriate node is displayed when control is passed back to a higher level of **BROWSE** from the next lowest level. When a call is made to a lower level of **BROWSE**, the first member of the current tree is chopped off so that the deeper level can look at its own portion of the tree. But processing in the original calling level is not stopped, merely suspended. If and when the lower level stops, then control returns to the next highest level with that level's version of the tree intact. Remember that because of our recursive definition of tree structure, any level of the tree can act as a whole tree.

If you want to use **BROWSE**, you first must create a tree with **EXPERT.CONSTRUCTOR**. If you created the electricity expert we used as an earlier example, then you can look at it by typing

```
BROWSE :ELECTRICITY
```

Spend some time browsing through trees, and you will come to appreciate the power of recursion. It is worth your while to understand this procedure completely. Draw some of your own trees on paper, use **EXPERT.CONSTRUCTOR** to build them into lists, and then tour them with **EXPLORE** and **BROWSE**.

These general-purpose tools can be used to create expert systems on almost any subject. They have weaknesses, however; for instance, they can be used only with binary-branching systems. It is not hard to modify them to work with trees with more than two branches per node, though, as long as the branching is consistent. Instead of the binary-tree list representing a parent node and two children, for example, it is easy to imagine a list representing a parent node and four children, for a total of five members in the list.

The expert systems that are created with these tools, like experts everywhere, think they know everything; they don't attempt to learn anything from the user. Harold Abelson, in his book *Apple Logo* (Appendix D), develops a game called *animal* that not only keeps its knowledge in a binary tree, much as we do here, but also has the ability to learn—to add to its knowledge tree.

Also, trees are very weak when it comes to representing networks such as the one shown in figure 6.13, in which several paths lead to the same destination. Networks might be best represented in Logo with property lists, in which each node has properties that name its neighbors. (Chapter 5 discussed the use of property lists, although not this application.) Indeed, you can use property lists to represent trees with variable numbers of branches by defining properties such as **LEFTCHILD**, **RIGHTCHILD**, and **PARENT**. Such a project is beyond the scope of this chapter, but it is no more difficult than other projects in this book.

One significant modification we can make to this system is to change **EXPLORE** and **BROWSE** so that, instead of simply printing the contents of each node, they **RUN** the node. This opens up a multitude of possibilities. For instance, each node can be a list of procedures that graphically illustrate the question or explain how to find the answer. The final

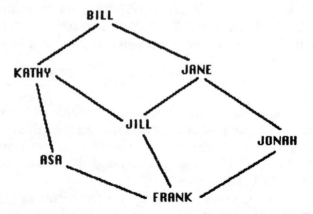

Figure 6.13
A network

act of any node should still be to ask a yes-or-no question to direct the next move. A node also can contain a command to **EXPLORE** some other tree. That way, expert systems can be assembled separately and then combined into other, more comprehensive systems. (This is possible because of Logo's ability to treat data as a program.) Essentially, this sets up a program control structure that is a tree. This change is far-reaching, but there is not enough space in this book to discuss it fully. The reader is left with the modified **EXPLORE** and **BROWSE** and encouragement to investigate their use:

```
TO EXPLORE :TREE
IF EMPTYP :TREE
     [STOP]
RUN FIRST :TREE    ; NOTE CHANGE HERE
IF READCHAR = "Y   ; CHECK USER RESPONSE
     [EXPLORE LEFT.BRANCH :TREE]    ; YES
     [EXPLORE RIGHT.BRANCH :TREE]    ; NO
END


TO BROWSE :TREE
IF EMPTYP :TREE
     [PRINT [END OF BRANCH] STOP]
RUN FIRST :TREE    ; NOTE CHANGE HERE
MAKE "DIRECTION FILTER [Y N U] RC
IF :DIRECTION = "Y
     [BROWSE LEFT.BRANCH :TREE]
     [IF :DIRECTION = "N
          [BROWSE RIGHT.BRANCH :TREE]
          ; ELSE, MUST BE UP
          [STOP]    ; RETURN TO NEXT HIGHEST NODE
     ]
BROWSE :TREE    ; PICK UP WHERE YOU LEFT OFF
END
```

TREE SORTING

Trees, along with being beautiful to look at and good for structuring knowledge in expert systems, are excellent for storing sorted data when speedy retrieval is a prime concern. Although the sorting routines that we develop here are not terribly fast, you will see that once the sorted tree has been set up, the search routines go much faster than with data sorted into sequential lists. This is because every time the tree search routine makes a comparison and a decision, as many as half the available choices are eliminated from further scrutiny.

We can start with an unordered list of data (we use numbers here, but the modification to use words is not difficult). Elements of this list are picked off one by one and placed in a developing tree according to the following three rules:

1   If the current node is empty, put the number at that node.

2   If the number is less than the current node of the tree, try to place the number in the left branch below the node.

3   If the number is greater than or equal to the current node, try to place the number in the right branch below the node.

These three rules are implemented in a Logo procedure called **INSERT**:

```
TO INSERT :ITEM :TREE
IF EMPTYP :TREE
     [OUTPUT (LIST :ITEM [] [])]     ; NEW NODE
IF :ITEM < FIRST :TREE
     [OUTPUT (LIST FIRST :TREE
                      INSERT :ITEM
                          LEFT.BRANCH :TREE
                  RIGHT.BRANCH :TREE
             )
      ]
     ; ELSE GREATER THAN
     [OUTPUT (LIST FIRST :TREE
                 LEFT.BRANCH :TREE
                 INSERT :ITEM
                      RIGHT.BRANCH :TREE
             )
      ]
END
```

As this procedure goes through its checks, it carries the unused portions of the tree along through each level of recursion until an empty node is finally found. Then the new number is added to the end of that branch. Notice that when the new member is added it also brings along two empty lists to mark the new end of that branch. All three of the output situations result in three-member lists, in much the same fashion as with **TREE.BUILDER** from the earlier part of this chapter. The ultimate output of **INSERT** is the entire tree (in list form) that was input, with a new member tacked onto the appropriate branch. Repeated calls to **INSERT** create a sorted tree.

Once **INSERT** is defined, the task of sorting a list of numbers into a tree becomes the task of **INSERT**ing the **FIRST** member of the list into an already sorted **BUTFIRST** of the list. In this case you may not even have to fully understand how the recursion works because the logic of the recursive definition is so strong that you come to the solution intuitively, knowing that it just has to work.

When you first start working with recursion, you may spend hours analyzing all the steps of a procedure down through every level to convince yourself that it indeed works. Once you have endured that journey into the underworld, then you can concentrate on the more abstract thinking that recursion allows. Rather than worrying about the particulars of how the recursion is going to keep track of all the inputs and levels, you are freed to think about the problem in its simplest terms. At a certain point in your experience, it will be sufficient to say that a tree branch is equivalent to a tree on the next lowest level. Sometimes the solutions to recursively defined problems are so simple that they are startling.

```
TO TREESORT :NUMBERLIST
IF EMPTYP :NUMBERLIST
     [OUTPUT []]
OUTPUT INSERT FIRST :NUMBERLIST
               TREESORT BUTFIRST :NUMBERLIST
END
```

The structure of this procedure is very similar to that of the insert-sorting procedure described in chapter 4. **TREESORT** uses a different insertion method but similarly assumes that it is inserting into an already sorted list. With the sorting defined this way, the last member of the list is actually the first one to be sorted into the tree (which is just **[]** at that point). Then the recursive levels back up through the list, **INSERT**ing each member, until the first member is the last one to be sorted into the tree. Try it out with

```
PRINT TREESORT [6 3 9 5 1 8 6 4]
```

which gives

```
[4 [1 [] [3] [] []]] [6 [5 [] []] [8 [6 [] [] [9
[] []]]]]
```

(which is the list form of the tree in figure 6.14). Or try it out with

```
MAKE "TREE.LIST TREESORT [6 3 9 5 1 8 6 4]
```

You can see that one side of the tree in figure 6.14 has more members than the other. For sorting and searching purposes, it is generally best to have what is called a *balanced tree*. To achieve this you try to get an uppermost node that is close to the midpoint of your data so that the data items are evenly distributed to the right and left as they are sorted.

It is not difficult to imagine using these procedures to sort words into trees. **INSERT** can be changed so that it uses the procedure **LESS.THAN**, developed in chapter 4, rather than < as the test in the fourth line. It is also a minor task to convert **INSERT** so that it sorts according to particular key fields of data kept as lists. For instance, suppose that you want to keep track of information for an index, much

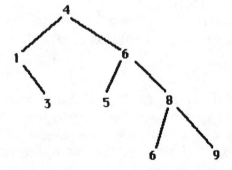

Figure 6.14
The tree corresponding to
TREESORT [6 3 9 5 1 8 6 4]

as we did in chapter 5 with property lists. This information can be kept in a tree, each node of which has the following structure:

```
[KEY WORD [PAGE NUMBERS]]
```

An example of such a node is

```
[FORWARD [34 35 36 88]]
```

When data are inserted, the tree is sorted according to the key-word value by the **LESS.THAN** procedure that we developed in chapter 4. We can write a new procedure, **UPDATE**, that is an adaptation of **INSERT**. **UPDATE** takes an existing tree (which might be **[ ]** to begin with) and inserts a new node like the one shown above. At each node, the key word of the current root node and the key word of the new node are compared. When they are the same, then the page numbers of the new node are added to the list of page numbers at the current root node. This structure can be referred to as a *dangling tree*, for each node can have a variable-length list of page numbers attached to it as well as the familiar right and left branches. This dynamic structure can be used to cross-reference the text of a program as well as to index books. In fact, with very little tinkering you can use this structure to keep track of almost any information that does not associate in chunks of consistent size.

As the search for matching keys proceeds, it is directed to the right or left branches of the tree, depending on whether the key of the new node is greater or less than the key of the root node, much as with **INSERT**. If the search for a matching key comes to the empty list that signifies a terminal branch, then the new node is added to the end of the branch and becomes a new terminal node.

We can define a couple of short procedures to clarify our assumptions about the data:

```
TO ROOT :TREE
OUTPUT FIRST :TREE
END

TO KEY :NODE
OUTPUT FIRST :NODE
END

TO DATA :NODE
OUTPUT LAST :NODE
END
```

Once we have defined these tools as well as **LESS.THAN** from chapter 4, **UPDATE** looks like this:

```
TO UPDATE :TREE :NEWNODE
IF EMPTYP :TREE    ; TERMINAL NODE
     [OUTPUT (LIST :NEWNODE [] [])]
IF KEY ROOT :TREE = KEY :NEWNODE    ; MATCHING NODE
     [OUTPUT (LIST (LIST KEY :NEWNODE
                              SENTENCE DATA ROOT :TREE
                                       DATA :NEWNODE
                        )
                   LEFT.BRANCH :TREE
                   RIGHT.BRANCH :TREE
              )
     ]
IF LESS.THAN (KEY :NEWNODE) (KEY ROOT :TREE)
     [OUTPUT (LIST ROOT :TREE
                   UPDATE LEFT.BRANCH :TREE
                          :NEWNODE
                   RIGHT.BRANCH :TREE
              )
     ]
; OTHERWISE PUT IT IN RIGHT BRANCH
     [OUTPUT (LIST ROOT :TREE
                   LEFT.BRANCH :TREE
                   UPDATE RIGHT.BRANCH :TREE
                          :NEWNODE
              )
     ]
END
```

You can see that this is very similar in form to **INSERT**. All the output statements result in three-member lists that maintain the list structure of the tree. This procedure can be used to build an index tree and then to update it. An entry that has not been put into the tree before is put at the end of the appropriate branch. An entry with a key word that is already in the tree has its data components added to the data of the node that contains that key word. This flexible data structure can be adapted for many purposes.

To use **UPDATE**, it is best to write a shell that adapts it to the particular situation. As an example, let's write a procedure to do an index for a book. We want a procedure that repeatedly asks for the key word and relevant page numbers. This is a good application for the dangling tree because more page numbers associate with some words than with others and also because the dangling tree's structure is suited to repeated entry of the same key word with various page numbers.

Before we define the shell, we need to define a global variable for the tree. We make the variable global so that it is saved to the disk with the rest of the workspace:

```
MAKE "TREE []

TO INDEX
TYPE [WORD>>>]
MAKE "WORD.TEMP FIRST READLIST
TYPE [PAGE NUMBERS>>>]
MAKE "PAGES.TEMP READLIST
MAKE "TREE UPDATE :TREE LIST :WORD.TEMP
                              :PAGES.TEMP

INDEX
END
```

This is not the best procedure in the world (you must use <control> **G** to stop it), but it should give you an idea of how to write a simple shell around **UPDATE** to help you enter data into the tree.

SEARCHING TREES ————————————————————

Once you have sorted your data into a tree list, you want to be able to get at certain items in the tree. Indeed, the real strength of tree-sorted lists is their speed of retrieval. The search strategy is similar to that used to construct the tree in the first place. Each node of the tree is checked to see if it matches the desired value. Again, as with the tree-forming procedure, there are three rules to follow:

1   If the value of the target matches the node value, then end the search and output the node.

2   If the value of the target is less than the node value, then call the search recursively with the left branch of the tree below the current node.

3   Otherwise search the right branch of the tree below the current node.

The resemblence of these rules to the rules that govern **INSERT** and **UPDATE** is not coincidental. Once these rules are formulated, the procedure comes easily:

```
TO TREESEARCH :ITEM :TREE
IF EMPTYP :TREE
      [OUTPUT []]    ; NOT FOUND
IF EQUALP :ITEM FIRST :TREE
      [OUTPUT FIRST :TREE]    ; FOUND
IF :ITEM < FIRST :TREE
      [OUTPUT TREESEARCH :ITEM
                         LEFT.BRANCH :TREE
      ]
      [OUTPUT TREESEARCH :ITEM
                         RIGHT.BRANCH :TREE
      ]
END
```

Assuming that you have created a sorted tree list called **TREELIST**, to use this procedure you type something like

```
PRINT TREESEARCH 6 :TREELIST
```

which prints the 6 if it is in the tree and nothing if it isn't. Like **INSERT**, this procedure is easily modified to deal with words or key elements of complex nodes. The changes that are needed are much the same as those discussed at the end of the previous section. The key word of each node entry can be matched with a key word supplied as a search image. Whenever the search word and the key word of the node match, then all the data associated with that node can be pulled out for further scrutiny.

The speed advantage of this procedure erodes if the tree in question is very unbalanced (with much more data to the right than to the left of the root node, or vice versa), but you will find that **TREESEARCH** is much faster in general than a search of a sequentially sorted list. Many commercial data-base programs rely on tree sorts and searches to give high performance with large amounts of data. The routines developed here will allow you to use these structures to great advantage in your own applications.

SUMMARY

This chapter has shown trees as visual forms, as expert systems, and as efficient data structures. Data trees are by definition recursive structures. It is hard to imagine creating tree procedures that do not use recursion, although it can probably be done.

Tree concepts can be implemented recursively in other languages, notably Pascal, but the implementation involves the use of pointers and is much less intuitive than in Logo. (Of course our procedures can be written in LISP, but doing them in LISP is almost the same thing as doing them in Logo.) This illustrates Logo's ability to give the programmer convenient ways of conceptualizing problem solutions that have to do less with the inner working of the computer than with familiar models of the situation. Also, once we have worked out our initial tools to translate tree structure into list structure, we are freed to think about possible applications for trees without having to worry about how the data can be represented internally. Once again, Logo programming creates tools and shells that allow the user to think in broad terms rather than be concerned with computer details.

Most of the procedures in this chapter utilize extensive recursion and accumulation of output. They can be hard to grasp the first (or even the twentieth) time through. If you are one of the few to whom the workings of recursion seem obvious, more power to you. If you are like most of the rest of us, then it may take a while for the ideas to click. Work with the routines and analyze their logic. Over and over again, watch trees being drawn on the screen. Create trees on paper, and them commit them to lists with **TREE.BUILDER**. When you have all but given up after your umpteenth recursive attempt at understanding recursion, you will at some point suddenly smile to yourself, reach for your pencil, and begin to jot down your own recursive routine.

7 PATTERN MATCHING

Pattern-Matching Procedures

LOOKUP

Creating Data Bases

Summary

In this chapter we shall develop procedures that match patterns and allow the use of *wildcard* characters for retrieval of data from a data base. Many of the concepts and tools introduced earlier in the book will be put to work here in an integrated project. The goal of this chapter is to create an address-book program that keeps a list of names and addresses that we can access in any way we choose by means of the program's pattern-matching procedures. We want to be able to get information like the names and addresses of all the people in the book who live in Vermont or the names and addresses of all the people in the book who are named Bill and who have a zip code of 97011. This data-base system must also be flexible enough to accommodate information other than names and addresses so that it can be used in applications other than the address-book sort. This project is a good introduction to Logo's applications to data bases. Our program does not rival commercial products for speed or power, but it does show some of the uses of pattern matching.

PATTERN-MATCHING PROCEDURES

To start off, we need to develop the pattern-matching tools that are at the heart of this project. As in most of this book, we are using a bottom-up programming style. It is just as feasible to practice top-down programming in Logo; for our purposes, however, it seems best to understand the lower-level tools first and then to build shells around them to create usable systems.

To check for a pattern match, our procedure looks at a *pattern* and an *assertion*. An *assertion* is a data object that is part of our data base, such as **[COLOR CANARY YELLOW]**. The *pattern* **[COLOR CANARY ?]** is a match for the assertion under certain predefined conditions. The pattern can contain a *wildcard* character that matches any item in the same relative position in the assertion. We shall use a question mark (**?**) in our procedure as the wildcard to match exactly one item in the assertion. This is an arbitrary choice, and other situations may dictate that another character be used instead.

Here are some examples of patterns, assertions, and the results we expect when we apply our pattern matcher to them:

pattern	*assertion*	*result*
[]	[]	true
[A B C]	[A B C]	true
[? B C]	[Z B C]	true
[? B C]	[[A B C] B C]	true
[? B C]	[A B C D]	false
[?]	[[A B C]]	true
[?]	[A B C]	false

From these examples we can generalize to rules that define a match between a pattern and an assertion:

1   The pattern and the assertion match if they are equal (the most obvious rule). This rule applies when both the pattern and the assertion are empty, by the way.

2   The pattern and the assertion do not match if they are of unequal lengths. Remember that the length of a list is measured only one level deep. For example, these two lists both have three members:

```
[BILL GAIL [SALLY JEAN HOWARD]]
[RALPH SARAH [DAVID JOYCE]]
```

3   If the first element of the pattern is **?** or if the first element of the pattern is equal to the first element of the assertion, then the **BUTFIRST**s of the pattern and assertion are checked for a match.

On the basis of these rules we can write the first pattern matcher:

```
TO MATCH :PATTERN :ASSERTION
IF EQUALP :PATTERN :ASSERTION
    [OUTPUT "TRUE]   ; OBVIOUS CASE
IF OR EMPTYP :PATTERN
    EMPTYP :ASSERTION
    [OUTPUT "FALSE]   ; UNEQUAL LENGTH
```

```
     IF OR EQUALP FIRST :PATTERN "?
          EQUALP FIRST :PATTERN FIRST :ASSERTION
        ; SO FAR SO GOOD, CHECK THE REST
        [OUTPUT MATCH BUTFIRST :PATTERN
                      BUTFIRST :ASSERTION
        ]
        ; ELSE QUIT NOW
        [OUTPUT "FALSE]
END
```

Try this procedure with some of the examples displayed above and some examples of your own until you understand its behavior and limitations. For instance, you can try something like

```
PRINT MATCH [FOO BAR ?] [FOO BAR SEAL]
```

An excellent way to see how this procedure is working is to put a debugging step into it to print out the current values of the pattern and the assertion as the procedure goes through recursive levels of execution. Adding the line

```
PRINT LIST :PATTERN :ASSERTION
```

as the first step of **MATCH** gives you a window into the inner working of the procedure. You can see how the inputs are whittled down and evaluated recursively. With this new line added, **MATCH** looks like this:

```
TO MATCH :PATTERN :ASSERTION
PRINT LIST :PATTERN :ASSERTION    ; PEEPHOLE
IF EQUALP :PATTERN :ASSERTION
     [OUTPUT "TRUE]   ; OBVIOUS CASE
IF OR EMPTYP :PATTERN
     EMPTYP :ASSERTION
     [OUTPUT "FALSE]    ; UNEQUAL LENGTH
IF OR EQUALP FIRST :PATTERN "?
     EQUALP FIRST :PATTERN FIRST :ASSERTION
     ; SO FAR SO GOOD, CHECK THE REST
     [OUTPUT MATCH BUTFIRST :PATTERN
                   BUTFIRST :ASSERTION
     ]
     ; ELSE QUIT NOW
     [OUTPUT "FALSE]
END
```

Figure 7.1 shows user interaction with **MATCH** now that the debugging peephole is installed. This kind of addition to a procedure can often help you understand difficult or subtle recursion.

In our address data base, this matching procedure could be used to check for all people named Jones by matching the pattern **[? JONES]** against assertions such as **[JOHN JONES]**, **[BILL JONES]**, and perhaps **[FRANK JOHNSON]**. But the procedure has weaknesses: one is that there is no way to match the assertions **[JOHN JONES]** and **[JOHN L. JONES]** with the same pattern. In the first case you need the pattern **[? JONES]**, and in the second, **[? ? JONES]**. Another limitation of this pattern matcher is that it cannot see wildcard characters if they are in sublists of the pattern, as in

```
PRINT MATCH [[? B C] D E] [[A B C] D E]
```

This example evaluates as **FALSE** even though you probably think it should not. This is because **MATCH** sees the first element of the pattern as the object **[? B C]** and does not delve into its makeup. **MATCH** never looks for a wildcard character in this sublist, so it returns **FALSE** because **[? B C]** is not equal, character for character, to **[A B C]**.

```
? PRINT MATCH [? B C] [A B C]
    [? B C] [A B C]
    [B C] [B C]
    TRUE
?
? PRINT MATCH [[?] B C] [[A] B C]
    [[?] B C] [[A] B C]
    FALSE
?
? PRINT MATCH [A B ?] [A B C D]
    [A B ?] [A B C D]
    [B ?] [B C D]
    [?] [C D]
    [] [D]
    FALSE
?
? PRINT MATCH [? JONES] [JOHN JONES]
    [? JONES] [JOHN JONES]
    [JONES] [JONES]
    TRUE
?
? PRINT MATCH [? JONES] [JOHN H JONES]
    [? JONES] [JOHN H JONES]
    [JONES] [H JONES]
    FALSE
?
```

Figure 7.1
Interaction with MATCH

Let's develop another pattern matcher to eliminate these two problems. To solve the first problem, we can use a second wildcard character, the asterisk (*), to match zero or more items in the same relative position in the assertion, so that **[A * C]** matches **[A C]**, **[A B C]**, **[A B D C]**, and **[A [B] [D E] X C]**. In our data base, **[* JONES]** now will match both **[JOHN JONES]** and **[JOHN L. JONES]**.

To solve the second problem, we can use the primitives **NOT** and **WORDP** to see if the first member of the pattern is a word or a list. **WORDP** is a predicate that is **TRUE** if its input is a word. If the first member of the pattern is a list, then we treat that list recursively and evaluate it with the pattern matcher before checking the rest of the pattern. This allows the pattern matcher to treat sublists separately and find buried wildcard characters in patterns like **[[A ? C] D E]**.

These two new abilities greatly increase the flexibility of the procedure. Note than in the line in **MATCH** that begins

```
IF OR EQUALP FIRST :PATTERN "?
```

the else clause is **[OUTPUT ''FALSE]**. In **MATCH2** there is no else clause in this line because the procedure goes on to check other possibilities:

```
TO MATCH2 :PATTERN :ASSERTION
PRINT LIST :PATTERN :ASSERTION    ; PEEPHOLE
IF EQUALP :PATTERN :ASSERTION
     [OUTPUT "TRUE]    ; OBVIOUS CASE
IF OR EMPTYP :PATTERN
      EMPTYP :ASSERTION
     [OUTPUT "FALSE]    ; UNEQUAL LENGTHS
IF NOT WORDP FIRST :PATTERN
     ; EVALUATE SUBLISTS
     [OUTPUT IF MATCH2 FIRST :PATTERN
                    FIRST :ASSERTION
          ; SUBLISTS MATCH, CHECK THE REST
          [OUTPUT MATCH2 BUTFIRST :PATTERN
                      BUTFIRST :ASSERTION
        ]
          ; SUBLISTS DON'T MATCH, QUIT NOW
          [OUTPUT "FALSE]
       ]
```

```
IF OR EQUALP FIRST :PATTERN "?
      EQUALP FIRST :PATTERN FIRST :ASSERTION
      ; SO FAR SO GOOD, CHECK THE REST
      [OUTPUT MATCH2 BUTFIRST :PATTERN
                      BUTFIRST :ASSERTION
         ]
IF EQUALP FIRST :PATTERN "*
      ; ASSUME IT MATCHES ZERO ELEMENTS
      [OUTPUT IF MATCH2 BUTFIRST :PATTERN
                        :ASSERTION
         [OUTPUT "TRUE]
         ; ASSUME IT MATCHES ONE ELEMENT
         [OUTPUT IF MATCH2 BUTFIRST :PATTERN
                           BUTFIRST :ASSERTION
            [OUTPUT "TRUE]
            ; MATCHES MORE THAN ONE
            [OUTPUT MATCH2 :PATTERN
                           BUTFIRST :ASSERTION
            ]
         ]
      ]
; NOTHING ELSE WORKED
OUTPUT "FALSE
END
```

The first change in **MATCH2** solves the problem of patterns with sublists. By using the statement **IF NOT WORDP FIRST :PATTERN**, the procedure now checks to see if the first element of the pattern is a word. If the first element of the pattern is a list, as in

```
MATCH2 [[? B C] D E] [[A B C] D E]
```

then **MATCH2** is called recursively with the first element of the pattern, **[? B C]**, and the first element of the assertion, **[A B C]**, as inputs. These two sublists are evaluated by another copy of **MATCH2** separately from the rest of the pattern and assertion. If the sublists match, then another copy of **MATCH2** is called, and this copy checks the rest of the pattern and assertion. If the sublists don't match, then the procedure stops and outputs **FALSE**. Here we are using nested conditional statements that output back out of the nesting levels all the way to the outermost layer. The sublists are treated by **MATCH2** in exactly the same way as the original two lists are, so the nesting of sublists can be arbitrarily deep, as in **[[[? B C] D] E]**. Such is the beauty of recursion.

The other change in **MATCH2** handles the new wildcard character, *. This part of the procedure is the most difficult to follow because it has to be able to match zero or more elements in the assertion with *. The strategy is to assume first of all that the * matches zero elements in the assertion, and drop the wildcard but leave the assertion intact. This combination is then tested recursively with a new copy of **MATCH2**. If the test comes up with a match, then **TRUE** is output. If this assumption does not give a match, then the else clause is called. The else clause invokes the second assumption, namely that the wildcard matches one element in the assertion.

If this is the case, the procedure treats the * in the same way **MATCH** treats the ?—by dropping the wildcard from the pattern and one element from the assertion and going around again to check the rest. If this assumption leads to a match for the entire assertion, then the result is **TRUE**. If this assumption does not lead to a match, then the next else clause is called, and it tries a third and final strategy.

The third strategy is to assume that the wildcard matches more than one element of the assertion. In this case the wildcard is retained, one element is dropped from the assertion, and **MATCH2** is called again to check the rest.

For example, if you are trying to match **[* B C]** against **[X Y B C]**, **MATCH2** first assumes that the wildcard character matches nothing in the assertion. It then drops the wildcard and tries to match **[B C]** against **[X Y B C]**. This does not yield a match, so the next assumption is invoked. Here the wildcard is assumed to match only the **X** in the assertion. The wildcard and the first element of the assertion (**X**) are dropped, and the procedure tries to match **[B C]** with **[Y B C]**, fails, and returns **FALSE**. At that point **MATCH2** tries the third assumption, keeps the wildcard, drops one element in the assertion, and then tries to match **[* B C]** against **[Y B C]**. This time around, it again assumes that the wildcard character matches zero elements in the assertion and tries to match **[B C]** with **[Y B C]**. The result is **FALSE**, so the next strategy is tried, namely assuming that the wildcard matches only one element in the assertion. This time, after dropping the wildcard and one element from the assertion, the procedure tries to match **[B C]** and **[B C]**. The result is **TRUE**, so the entire match is **TRUE**.

When **MATCH2** meets *, it tries different strategies until it finds one that makes the match **TRUE** or until there are no more characters in the assertion. **MATCH2** follows a path to a possible match until it yields **TRUE** or **FALSE**. If the outcome of a particular path is **FALSE**, then **MATCH2** tries another assumption and a different path toward matching. Although this gives the procedure lots of flexibility, it can cause the procedure to follow many unsuccessful matching paths, and it can require lots of processing to evaluate a match. Figure 7.2 shows user interaction with **MATCH2**, as fully disclosed by our debugging peephole. Study the examples and try some of your own to see how this backtracking strategy works.

```
? PRINT MATCH2 [* B C] [A B C]
   [* B C] [A B C]
   [B C] [A B C]
   [B C] [B C]
   TRUE
?
? PRINT MATCH2 [* B C] [A X B C]
   [* B C] [A X B C]
   [B C] [A X B C]
   [B C] [X B C]
   [* B C] [X B C]
   [B C] [X B C]
   [B C] [B C]
   TRUE
?
? PRINT MATCH2 [[A *] B C] [[A B] B C]
   [[A *] B C] [[A B] B C]
   [A *] [A B]
   [*] [B]
   [] [B]
   [] []
   [B C] [B C]
   TRUE
?
? PRINT MATCH2 [A B *] [A B C D]
   [A B *] [A B C D]
   [B *] [B C D]
   [*] [C D]
   [] [C D]
   [] [D]
   [*] [D]
   [] [D]
   [] []
   TRUE
?
? PRINT MATCH2 [* JONES] [JOHN H JONES]
   [* JONES] [JOHN H JONES]
   [JONES] [JOHN H JONES]
   [JONES] [H JONES]
   [* JONES] [H JONES]
   [JONES] [H JONES]
   [JONES] [JONES]
   TRUE
?
```

Figure 7.2
Interaction with MATCH2

One way to avoid some of the unsuccessful path searching in **MATCH2** is to add the statement

```
IF EQUALP :PATTERN [*]
     [OUTPUT "TRUE]    ; [*] MATCHES ALL
```

as the second statement of **MATCH2** (just after the debugging peephole). This is particularly efficient when patterns like **[A B *]** are matched against assertions like **[A B C D E F G]**. After two passes through **MATCH2**, the pattern and assertion in question are reduced to **[*]** and **[C D E F G]**. With the new step added, the procedure immediately recognizes a match, and processing stops. Without the new step, the procedure would have to go through the assertion one element at a time, trying different strategies, until the final match is verified. The new step creates an advantage when the * wildcard is the last element in the pattern list and it is matched against more than one element in the assertion. It also creates an advantage when **[*]** is used as a sublist in a pattern, as in

```
[[? JONES][*][DENVER][*][*]]
```

which would match any person with a last name of Jones living at any address in Denver. With the new step, **MATCH2** becomes **MATCH3**:

```
TO MATCH3 :PATTERN :ASSERTION
PRINT LIST :PATTERN :ASSERTION    ; PEEPHOLE
IF EQUALP :PATTERN [*]
     [OUTPUT "TRUE]    ; [*] MATCHES ALL
IF EQUALP :PATTERN :ASSERTION
     [OUTPUT "TRUE]    ; OBVIOUS CASE
IF OR EMPTYP :PATTERN
      EMPTYP :ASSERTION
     [OUTPUT "FALSE]    ; UNEQUAL LENGTHS
IF NOT WORDP FIRST :PATTERN
      ; EVALUATE SUBLISTS
     [OUTPUT IF MATCH3 FIRST :PATTERN
                       FIRST :ASSERTION
             ; SUBLISTS MATCH, CHECK THE REST
             [OUTPUT MATCH3 BUTFIRST :PATTERN
                            BUTFIRST :ASSERTION
              ]
             ; SUBLISTS DON'T MATCH, QUIT NOW
             [OUTPUT "FALSE]
      ]
```

```
IF OR EQUALP FIRST :PATTERN "?
        EQUALP FIRST :PATTERN FIRST :ASSERTION
      ; SO FAR SO GOOD, CHECK THE REST
      [OUTPUT MATCH3 BUTFIRST :PATTERN
                      BUTFIRST :ASSERTION
      ]
IF EQUALP FIRST :PATTERN "*
      ; ASSUME IT MATCHES ZERO ELEMENTS
      [OUTPUT IF MATCH3 BUTFIRST :PATTERN
                        :ASSERTION
            [OUTPUT "TRUE]
            ; ASSUME IT MATCHES ONE ELEMENT
            [OUTPUT IF MATCH3 BUTFIRST :PATTERN
                              BUTFIRST :ASSERTION
                  [OUTPUT "TRUE]
                  ; ASSUME IT MATCHES MORE THAN ONE
                  [OUTPUT MATCH3 :PATTERN
                                 BUTFIRST :ASSERTION
                  ]
            ]
      ]
; NOTHING ELSE WORKED
OUTPUT "FALSE
END
```

Figure 7.3 shows the workings of **MATCH2** and **MATCH3** in the same situations. You can see that sometimes **MATCH3** is more efficient, but not always.

At this point we have a usable pattern matcher, although you probably want to remove the peephole step before you put the pattern matcher into final use in the data-base application. This is the longest single Logo procedure that we have developed yet in this book. It uses nested conditional (if . . . then . . . else) statements and recursion to backtrack. One thing it does not do is find wildcard characters inside words that are inside lists, such as **[?ONES]**. To find wildcard characters in such positions, the procedure would need yet another level of checking that goes through each word in the pattern character by character. Such a change would make the whole process too slow for our particular application, but the change could be made without much difficulty if that capability were important.

```
PRINT MATCH2 [A B *] [A B C]
    [A B *] [A B C]
    [B *] [B C]
    [*] [C]
    [] [C]
    [] []
    TRUE

PRINT MATCH2 [A B *] [A B C D]
    [A B *] [A B C D]
    [B *] [B C D]
    [*] [C D]
    [] [C D]
    [] [D]
    [*] [D]
    [] [D]
    [] []
    TRUE

PRINT MATCH2 [A B * D] [A B C D]
    [A B * D] [A B C D]
    [B * D] [B C D]
    [* D] [C D]
    [D] [C D]
    [D] [D]
    TRUE

PRINT MATCH2 [* JONES] [JOHN H JONES]
    [* JONES] [JOHN H JONES]
    [JONES] [JOHN H JONES]
    [JONES] [H JONES]
    [* JONES] [H JONES]
    [JONES] [H JONES]
    [JONES] [JONES]
    TRUE
```

```
PRINT MATCH3 [A B *] [A B C]
    [A B *] [A B C]
    [B *] [B C]
    [*] [C]
    TRUE

PRINT MATCH3 [A B *] [A B C D]
    [A B *] [A B C D]
    [B *] [B C D]
    [*] [C D]
    TRUE

PRINT MATCH3 [A B * D] [A B C D]
    [A B * D] [A B C D]
    [B * D] [B C D]
    [* D] [C D]
    [D] [C D]
    [D] [D]
    TRUE

PRINT MATCH3 [* JONES] [JOHN H JONES]
    [* JONES] [JOHN H JONES]
    [JONES] [JOHN H JONES]
    [JONES] [H JONES]
    [* JONES] [H JONES]
    [JONES] [H JONES]
    [JONES] [JONES]
    TRUE
```

Figure 7.3
MATCH2 versus MATCH3

LOOKUP

Now that we have a pattern matcher that works, we need to put it to use. If we are given the list of data assertions **[[COLOR CANARY YELLOW] [COLOR CARDINAL RED] [COLOR BLUEBIRD BLUE]]**, we want to be able to go through that list and find information like the color of a canary (**[COLOR CANARY ?]**) and the names of all blue creatures in the list (**[COLOR ? BLUE]**). The information we want must be formulated as patterns with wildcards, and then the patterns must be checked against each element of the assertion list, with the matching elements singled out for further examination. For now, you must do the pattern translation manually, although later we shall automate that process with a Logo procedure. Once you have formulated a pattern, you can feed it to this **LOOKUP** procedure:

```
TO LOOKUP :PATTERN :DATALIST
IF EMPTYP :DATALIST
     [OUTPUT []]
IF MATCH3 :PATTERN FIRST :DATALIST
     [OUTPUT FPUT FIRST :DATALIST
                  LOOKUP :PATTERN
                         BUTFIRST :DATALIST
      ]
OUTPUT LOOKUP :PATTERN BUTFIRST :DATALIST
END
```

Now if you define some sort of assertion list, such as

```
MAKE "ASSERTIONS [[BROTHER.OF BILL JACK]
[SISTER.OF BILL SARA] [MOTHER.OF JACK JILL]
[MOTHER.OF BILL JILL] [HUSBAND.OF SARAH PHIL]]
```

you can begin to use **LOOKUP** by typing commands like the following:

```
PRINT LOOKUP [BROTHER.OF BILL ?] :ASSERTIONS
PRINT LOOKUP [BROTHER.OF *] :ASSERTIONS
PRINT LOOKUP [? SARAH PHIL] :ASSERTIONS
```

As **LOOKUP** goes through the assertions, it checks the first member each time to see if it matches the pattern. If it does, then the matching assertion is singled out for output with the **FPUT** command. The matching assertion is **FPUT** into whatever the final output of **LOOKUP** happens to be. Along the way, more assertion elements may be selected and put into the **FPUT** queue until the assertion list is empty and the final **[ ]** is output. At that point the waiting assertions are **FPUT** into this empty list, with the first one selected being the last one to be **FPUT**. We have used this method of accumulating output in many other procedures in this book, so it should be familiar to you by now. If there aren't any assertion elements that match the pattern, then the empty list is the final output, as you would expect.

Note that this is a low-level tool, in that it merely outputs a raw list of its findings. It needs to be conjoined with other procedures to make it usable by the naive. Let's incorporate **LOOKUP** into a shell that hides **LOOKUP**'s workings from the user and provides a layer of forgiving interaction that formulates the user's input into patterns and assertion lists acceptable to the low-level tool. Then the shell can massage the output of the tool into an easily readable form before passing it back to the user.

CREATING DATA BASES

For any sort of realistic application, you do not want to have to create your assertion lists by hand as we did in the previous section. We need some tools to help create lists of assertions.

The functions that are important to any data-base program are

1   Defining the fields that make up the records in a particular file. This makes the program flexible enough to be used in a number of different situations.

2   Adding data to these fields, one record at a time.

3   Deleting all the records that match a user-defined pattern.

4   Searching for and displaying records that match a user-defined pattern.

5   Saving the current body of data to disk for future use.

Taking these functions one at a time, we can define some procedures to implement our tools.

Defining Data Records

We can use a model from commercial data-base programs in which data are organized on three levels: the *file*, the *record*, and the *field*. For example, the *file* in your address book is the collection of all the names and addresses. A *record* in that file is the name and address of one person. A *field* in that record is the name, address, or zip code of that person.

To see these abstractions as Logo data objects, look at the following examples. The file can be

```
[[[JOHN JONES][5 FOO ST.][FOOVILLE][MA][02113]]
[[BILL JONES][7 BAR ST.][BARVILLE][CA][92118]]]
```

A record in that file is, for instance,

```
[[JOHN JONES][5 FOO ST.][FOOVILLE][MA][02113]]
```

A field is

```
[5 FOO ST.]
```

With these structures in mind, we can define some tools to build Logo objects that contain data assertions. We want these structures to be flexible, so we allow the user to define the field names that make up the records. Our procedure prompts the user for field names and builds a list of them. This list defines the structure of a record and acts as a guide for the other procedures that need to handle the records one field at a time:

```
TO GETFIELDS
LOCAL "INPUT     ; DECLARE LOCAL VARIABLE
TYPE [FIELD NAME>>>]
MAKE "INPUT READLIST
IF EMPTYP :INPUT
     [OUTPUT []]     ; ALL DONE
     [OUTPUT FPUT :INPUT GETFIELDS]
END
```

The user enters field names one by one after the prompt, hitting <return> after each entry. When all the fields have been entered, a simple <return> signals the procedure that the user is done. The list created by this procedure looks something like this:

```
[[NAME][STREET][CITY][STATE][ZIP]]
```

or this:

```
[[ELEMENT][ATOMIC NUMBER][ATOMIC WEIGHT]
[MELTING POINT]]
```

This procedure must be used with a **MAKE** command to bind its output list to a global variable available to the rest of the procedures in the workspace. To keep the value of your field definition available, use

```
MAKE "FIELDNAMES GETFIELDS
```

Thereafter, you can use the list of field names by typing **:FIELDNAMES**.

This tool can be incorporated into a friendly shell that communicates with the user and takes care of the variable assignments so that record format that is entered is not lost. First, to define a new-record format, we can make a procedure **DEFINE.FILE**:

```
TO DEFINE.FILE
PRINT [WARNING!!!]
PRINT [DEFINING A NEW FILE WILL]
PRINT [ERASE ANY FILES IN MEMORY.]
PRINT [DO YOU WANT TO DO THIS? Y OR N]
IF NOT EQUALP READCHAR "Y
     [STOP]    ; DON'T DO IT.
ERNS    ; ERASE ALL VARIABLES
MAKE "DATALIST []    ; INITIALIZE FILE
PRINT [] PRINT []
MAKE "FIELDS GETFIELDS
PRINT []
PRINT [DEFINITION COMPLETE]
GO.ON?
END

TO GO.ON?
TYPE [PRESS RETURN TO GO ON...]
MAKE "GO.ON READLIST
END
```

This system allows only one data file in memory at a time, so defining a new file erases the old one. The procedure first warns the user of this fact and then asks if the user indeed wants to define a new file. If the user gets cold feet and answers no, then the procedure terminates and gives the user a chance to save the current file, or whatever. If the user answers yes, then all variables in the workspace are erased with the **ERNS** (*erase names*) command. Then a new empty list, **DATALIST**, is created for the data, and a new list of field names is created with the **GETFIELDS** procedure that we developed earlier. The list of field names is assigned to the global variable **FIELDS**. **GO.ON?** is a short tool that waits for the user to press <return>. This little procedure, like so many in Logo, is easy to write and makes for code that is much more readable than it would otherwise be.

Adding Data

Once we have defined the names of the fields in a record, we can fill those fields with the data that are to be part of our assertion data base. We can write a routine to go through the list of field names and prompt the user for the data for each one. The data are then put into a nested list that has the same structure as the list of field names:

```
TO GETDATA :FIELDLIST
IF EMPTYP :FIELDLIST
     [OUTPUT []]
TYPE SENTENCE FIRST :FIELDLIST [>>>]
OUTPUT FPUT READLIST   ; USER DATA
          GETDATA BUTFIRST :FIELDLIST
END
```

Here again you can see how **FPUT** is used to accumulate data until the final empty list is output. The output of this procedure looks something like this:

```
[[JILL JONES][123 HAT RD.][MALCOM][IOWA][50113]]
```

or this:

```
[[HELIUM][2][4][-250 K]]
```

Now we have the tools to define a record and fill its fields with assertions. Because **GETDATA** merely outputs its result, we need to write a shell around **GETDATA** to assign the user's input to the global variable **DATALIST**, which contains all the data that the user supplies to fill in the blanks in the record format:

```
TO ADD
MAKE "DATALIST FPUT GETDATA :FIELDS
               :DATALIST
PRINT []
GO.ON?
END
```

This procedure relies upon the fact that **:DATALIST** and **:FIELDS** are defined globally by **DEFINE.FILE** when the file is initialized. The tool we defined previously, **GETDATA**, is called with the global value of **:FIELDS** as its input. It steps through this list of field names and gets data for each one. This list of assertions is then **FPUT** into the global list of records, **:DATALIST**.

Deleting Data

Next, we want to be able to delete a record or records that match a user-defined pattern. To do this, we first need a procedure that asks the user to define what he or she wants from a record and then translates that into a pattern that works with our pattern matcher. The user is prompted for each field in the record format. The user may enter a literal assertion such as **[JOHN JONES]**, enter a particular pattern such as **[? JONES]** or **[* JONES]**, or just hit <return> if it doesn't matter what is in that field. For example, if the user wants to define a pattern that matches the record in an address data base of anyone who is named Jones and lives in Arkansas, then the user enters **[* JONES]** for the name field, <return> for the street and city fields, **ARKANSAS** for the state field, and <return> for the zip field. That creates this pattern list:

```
[[* JONES][*][*][ARKANSAS][*]]
```

Keeping all this in mind, let's write a pattern-definition tool:

```
TO GETPATTERN :FIELDNAMES
LOCAL "INPUT
IF EMPTYP :FIELDNAMES
     [OUTPUT []]
TYPE SENTENCE FIRST :FIELDNAMES [>>>]
MAKE "INPUT READLIST
IF EMPTYP :INPUT         ; USER SAYS
     [OUTPUT FPUT [*]    ; ANYTHING OK HERE
               GETPATTERN BUTFIRST :FIELDNAMES
        ]
OUTPUT FPUT :INPUT GETPATTERN BUTFIRST :FIELDNAMES
END
```

This procedure uses a by now familiar accumulation method for creating a list of user-supplied field patterns. When the user simply presses <return> for a field instead of giving a pattern, then the procedure assumes that the contents of that field can be anything and thus supplies the **[*]** wildcard to the pattern list. Otherwise, the input of the user is put into the list just as it was typed in.

Now that the user can define a pattern on a field-by-field basis, we can move on to the procedure for deleting any arbitrary pattern from a file of records:

```
TO DELETE
PRINT [PLEASE DEFINE THE PATTERN]
PRINT [TO BE DELETED.]
PRINT []
LOCAL "PATTERN
MAKE "PATTERN GETPATTERN :FIELDS
MAKE "DATALIST DELETE.AUX :PATTERN :DATALIST
PRINT []
GO.ON?
END


TO DELETE.AUX :PATTERN :LIST
IF EMPTYP :LIST
    [OUTPUT []]
IF MATCH3 :PATTERN FIRST :LIST
    [OUTPUT DELETE.AUX :PATTERN    ; DROP ITEM
                        BUTFIRST :LIST
    ]
OUTPUT FPUT FIRST :LIST   ; KEEP ITEM
            DELETE.AUX :PATTERN
                        BUTFIRST :LIST
END
```

DELETE first of all asks the user to define the pattern of the records to be deleted. Remember that the tool **GETPATTERN** asks for information on a field-by-field basis. Once the user has defined the pattern, then that pattern is fed into **DELETE.AUX** together with the global value of **:DATALIST**. **DELETE.AUX** steps through the list of assertions and compares each one to the pattern. If there is a match, then that assertion is dropped. If there is no match, then the assertion is kept. This process continues until all the assertions in **:DATALIST** have been checked against the pattern. The final output of **DELETE.AUX** is made into the new global value of **:DATALIST**.

Actually, the pattern list generated by **GETPATTERN** is first put into a local varible before being passed to **DELETE.AUX**. This is done for the sake of readability. In fact, the output of **GETPATTERN** can be passed directly to **DELETE.AUX** with the command

```
MAKE "DATALIST DELETE.AUX GETPATTERN :FIELDNAMES
                             :DATALIST
```

This method does not require the declaration of a local variable, but otherwise it offers no significant advantage. Many experienced Logo programmers prefer this compact style, however, because it is more direct and elegant.

Finding Data

Next, we can search for records that match a user-defined pattern. The search function is similar to the delete function in that it asks the user to define a pattern and then goes into the list of assertions to look for matches. In this case, however, assertions that match are accumulated rather than dropped:

```
TO SEARCH
PRINT [PLEASE DEFINE THE PATTERN]
PRINT [FOR WHICH TO SEARCH.]
PRINT []
LOCAL "PATTERN
MAKE "PATTERN GETPATTERN :FIELDS
PRINT [] PRINT []
DISPLAY LOOKUP :PATTERN :DATALIST
PRINT []
GO.ON?
END

TO DISPLAY :LIST
IF EMPTYP :LIST
     [PRINT [THAT'S ALL FOLKS] STOP]
PRETTYPRINT FIRST :LIST
DISPLAY BUTFIRST :LIST
END
```

```
TO PRETTYPRINT :LIST
IF EMPTYP :LIST
     [PRINT [] STOP]
PRINT FIRST :LIST
PRETTYPRINT BUTFIRST :LIST
END
```

Starting at the top, you can see that **SEARCH** uses **GETPATTERN** to define the pattern for which the user wishes to serach. Then **LOOKUP**, which was defined earlier in the chapter, takes this pattern and applies it to the list of data assertions, accumulating and finally outputting all the assertions that match the pattern. This list is handed to **DISPLAY**, which picks out records one at a time (as there may be more than one record that matches the search pattern) and hands them to **PRETTYPRINT**. Here each record is printed out with each field on a separate line.

Just as the output of **GETPATTERN** can be passed directly to **DELETE.AUX**, so the output of **GETPATTERN** does not have to be assigned to the local variable before being passed to **LOOKUP**. The call to **LOOKUP** can be

```
DISPLAY LOOKUP GETPATTERN :FIELDS
               :DATALIST
```

Saving Data

Finally, we can save the data base onto disk so that it can be used again. Because there are as yet no standard ways to create and maintain sequential or random-access disk files in Logo, we need to save the entire workspace, including procedures and global variables. This is wasteful of disk space, and it underscores one of Logo's weaknesses. Newer versions of Logo are adding primitives that allow for more sophisticated file access, but since there is still no standard for these functions, our crude method will have to do for now. You are encouraged to look into the documentation of your version of Logo to investigate provisions for disk input and output. If you find that your version has these capabilities, then it is worthwhile for you to adapt the data-base procedures so that you can take advantage of them.

This next procedure asks the user for a file name and then saves the entire contents of the workspace onto the disk with that file name:

```
TO DISKSAVE
TYPE [FILENAME>>>]
SAVE FIRST READLIST
PRINT []
GO.ON?
END
```

You can see how this procedure takes advantage of Logo's ability to use input directly (wihout having to put it into a variable first). Note also that the procedure does not check to see if there is already a disk file of the same name on the disk. Neither Dr. Logo nor Apple Logo allows you to save a disk file if there is already a file with that name on the disk; you have to choose another name for your file or erase the file that already exists on the disk. Other versions of Logo may or may not write over files with the same name. This is another area in which there is no standard.

The Menu Shell

Now that we have our five main functions defined, let's put a menu shell around them all. This menu will guide the user to all the functions of the system:

```
TO MENU
CLEARTEXT
PRINT [DATA BASE SYSTEM]
PRINT []
PRINT [1. DEFINE A NEW FILE]
PRINT [2. ADD A RECORD]
PRINT [3. DELETE RECORDS]
PRINT [4. SEARCH FOR RECORDS]
PRINT [5. SAVE TO DISK]
PRINT [6. QUIT]
PRINT []
TYPE [CHOOSE NUMBER OF YOUR CHOICE>>>]
PROCESS FIRST READLIST
MENU
END
```

```
TO PROCESS :INPUT
IF :INPUT = "1 [CLEARTEXT DEFINE.FILE]
IF :INPUT = "2 [CLEARTEXT ADD]
IF :INPUT = "3 [CLEARTEXT DELETE]
IF :INPUT = "4 [CLEARTEXT SEARCH]
IF :INPUT = "5 [CLEARTEXT DISKSAVE]
IF :INPUT = "6 [CLEARTEXT QUIT]
END


TO QUIT
PRINT [DO YOU REALLY WANT TO QUIT? Y OR N]
IF EQUALP READCHAR "Y
     [THROW "TOPLEVEL]
END
```

QUIT uses **THROW "TOPLEVEL** to break out of the recursive loop in **MENU** and stop the whole program, returning control to the command prompt of the Logo interpreter.

At this point you can run the whole system from **MENU** if you have defined the following procedures in this chapter:

```
MATCH3
LOOKUP
GETFIELDS
GETDATA
DEFINE.FILE
GO.ON?
ADD
GETPATTERN
DELETE
DELETE.AUX
SEARCH
DISPLAY
PRETTYPRINT
DISKSAVE
MENU
PROCESS
QUIT
```

Remember to remove the debugging peephole from **MATCH3** before using **MATCH3** in this application. Otherwise your screen will fill with a display of the inner working of the pattern matcher.

SUMMARY ———————————————————————————————

This data-base system is far from complete. It cannot sort or edit its data, and it has no provision for directing output to a printer. Also, the lack of standard disk-file primitives hampers its use for serious applications with large amounts of data. But in spite of all this, it shows how Logo can be used to create a flexible and friendly system for managing data. You can see how the different functions of the system are created individually and then put together with the menu shell. The lower-level manipulations are hidden from the ultimate user by layers of tools and interactive shell procedures. You can modify the features discussed or incorporate your own into the system with little trouble by adding them to the menu shell. This chapter also shows how pattern matching can be used to facilitate flexible data retrieval. There are many other uses for this type of data-base system besides maintaining names and addresses. You are encouraged to dream up your own application and to try out some of the concepts presented here.

APPENDIX A: LOGO FUNDAMENTALS REVIEW

The System

The Parts of a Logo Procedure

Dots

Global and Local Variables

If . . . Then . . . Else Statements

Repetition

Recursion

Procedures That Output

Summary

This appendix presents the fundamental concepts of Logo in a systematic and abstract manner. It is in direct contrast to the body of the book, which presents the elements of Logo in the context of problem-solving situations. It is best to learn Logo through problem-solving experience, so this appendix is most appropriately used for reference. As Alan Kay has said, "The world of the symbolic can be dealt with effectively only when the repetitious aggregation of concrete instances becomes boring enough to motivate exchanging them for a single abstraction." Logo is built on this notion that learning progresses from the concrete and experiential to the abstract.

Logo is a computer-programming language created in the early 1970s as a tool to allow children to control powerful computers and explore ideas about problem solving. At the time, its advocates ran counter to the conventional wisdom by maintaining that, in order to have productive encounters with computers, children actually need more powerful computing resources than do adults. Logo thus was first implemented on large research computers. Only since the early 1980s have small personal computers been powerful enough to run Logo.

Because of its historical use in education, Logo has the reputation of being a kiddie language. Nothing could be further from the truth. Logo is, in fact, so easy to learn that it has been successfully taught to kindergartners, but it is easy to grasp precisely because of its great power. Most people tend to focus on turtle graphics as the sum and total of what Logo can do. But beyond turtle graphics there is a rich set of commands for manipulating text and numbers.

THE SYSTEM

Logo has been implemented on many different computers, but most versions of Logo have the following features:

1   *The command interpreter.* Logo is an interpreted language. It executes commands immediately when you type them in. This allows quick feedback and easy learning, but it does make the system slower than do languages that use compilers. Someday there may be versions of Logo that include compilers, thus allowing a person to write and debug programs in the interpreter and then feed the procedures to a compiler to gain the speed that compilers give. (This has been done for LISP, Logo's parent language, so it can be done for Logo.)

2 *Primitives.* These are the commands that are built into Logo and are available to the user at system startup. Different versions may feature additional primitives, but there is a core of commands that is common to all Logo systems. These primitives are used to control the system. Examples of primitives are **FORWARD**, **RIGHT**, **CLEARSCREEN**, **FIRST**, **BUTFIRST**, **PRINT**, and **SENTENCE**.

3 *Procedures.* Logo allows and even encourages the user to combine his or her own selections of primitives into procedures that can then be named and used to control the system. For example, if you want to write a greeting on the screen, you need to use the **CLEARTEST** and **PRINT** primitives. You can combine these commands into a procedure and name it **GREETING**:

```
TO GREETING
CLEARTEXT
PRINT [HELLO THERE]
END
```

Once this procedure has been defined in this way, it is sufficient for the user to type **GREETING** to execute all the commands in its definition. In a sense, writing procedures extends the vocabulary of the language to include new words. This important feature of Logo is the key to its power as a problem-solving tool. Problems can be attacked in small pieces and the individual solutions encoded as procedures. These procedures can later be combined to give an overall solution.

4 *The editor.* Most versions of Logo allow access to a full-screen editor to facilitate the modification of procedures. This makes it very easy for a person to write a procedure, test it out by running it immediately with the interpreter, and then go back into the editor to make the necessary modifications. This editor generally resides in memory, so that switching from the interpreter to the editor is quick and easy and causes minimal interruption of the problem-solving process.

THE PARTS OF A LOGO PROCEDURE

It is probably using a misnomer to refer to Logo *programs* in the same way as you refer to *programs* in BASIC. In BASIC and many other computer languages, a solution to a problem is encoded in one long series of instructions, often with sequential line numbers. In Logo, however, a solution to a problem is most often expressed as a collection of procedures that call upon each other to solve various sections of the problem. Often, there is a single procedure that initiates the overall problem solution, but its main job is to call the other procedures into action.

With that in mind, we can look at a Logo *procedure*, the main component of a problem solution. Figure A.1 shows a sample Logo procedure with its parts labeled. You can see that the first line of a Logo procedure is the *title line*. The title of a procedure always starts with **TO** because you are teaching the computer how *to* do something. The word that follows **TO** is the *procedure name*. You use this name when you want to run the procedure. The name you choose must not be the name of a primitive and must not contain any spaces.

Also on the title line you may put *inputs*, although they are optional. When you do put an input on the title line, Logo expects to see some extra information when you use the procedure. For instance, in the example shown in figure A.1, the input is **:SIZE** (read as *dots size*). You can see that **:SIZE** also shows up later in the body of the procedure. If **SQUARE** is defined as in figure A.1, you use it by typing something like

```
SQUARE 45
```

The number 45 is used wherever **:SIZE** occurs in the procedure: the command **FORWARD :SIZE** thus becomes **FORWARD 45**. Using different values next to **SQUARE** as input causes those values to be substituted into the procedure. Giving an input to a procedure is like reserving space where you can later put a number or text to be used by the

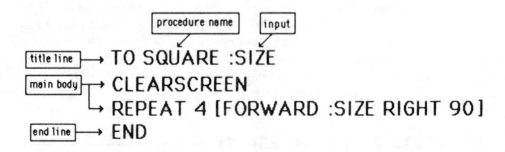

Figure A.1
A Logo procedure

commands in the body of the procedure. This makes procedures flexible—able to perform a variety of tasks. Chapter 1 discusses in detail how to write procedures with inputs.

The *main body* of the procedure can be made up of any commands that Logo normally understands. These include primitives and other procedures that you have defined. Herein lies the enormous power and flexibility of Logo. You can create customized procedures that you can then use in other procedures for further problem solving.

Finally, the last line (*end line*) of a Logo procedure definition must be the word **END** all by itself.

DOTS

Many people new to Logo are confused by the use of Logo's colon, the so-called *dots*. The colon is an abbreviated way of saying *the value of*. For instance, **:SIZE** means *the value of the variable named SIZE*.

In Logo, a word such as **SIZE** can have many different meanings. First of all, it can be a literal string of letters and digits, as when used in **"SIZE**. The leading quotation marks tell the Logo interpreter that you want the actual letters **S**, **I**, **Z**, and **E**. This notation is useful when you want to print a literal message: you can use an instruction like **PRINT "SIZE**. Note that there are no following quotation marks. The quotation marks are a prefix operator, just like other Logo primitives. In the same way as **FORWARD** is a primitive that takes a number as an input, as in **FORWARD 100**, the set of opening quotation marks is a primitive that takes a string of characters, as in **"FOOBAR**.

Second, the word **SIZE** can have a value associated with it, or bound to it. This value is accessed by using **:SIZE**, the value of **SIZE**. You can bind values to words by two methods: using words as inputs to procedures, as shown in the previous section, and using words with the **MAKE** command, as explained in the next section on global and local variables.

Third, the word **SIZE** can also be used as the name of a procedure. To assign this meaning to **SIZE**, you use it without the leading quotation marks or dots. When Logo encounters a word that does not have leading quotation marks or dots (or square brackets to mark a list), then it assumes that the word is the name of a primitive or procedure and tries to execute it.

Finally, a word may have properties associated with it. For instance, **SIZE** can have properties such as **MAXIMUM** and **MINIMUM**. Properties are created and examained by the primitives **PPROP** and **GPROP**. This topic is covered in detail in chapter 5.

Figure A.2 shows a word and all the meanings that can be assigned to it. To summarize, the value of a word is accessed with dots, the actual word itself is accessed by leading quotation marks, and the procedure definition is accessed by the word with no leading punctuation.

GLOBAL AND LOCAL VARIABLES

As mentioned in the previous section, there are two ways to create variables in Logo. One way is to write procedures with inputs; a temporary local variable is created to hold each input, each time the procedure is run. When the procedure finishes, the temporary variable is lost. Each procedure keeps its own personal library of input variables, so that two procedures can use the same name for their inputs and the values for the inputs are not confused with each other. This is a very important point to keep in mind when you are programming in Logo.

Because procedures keep their inputs local and do not confuse them with other variables of the same name, it is easy in Logo to program in modules. You do not have to worry about whether input names used in one procedure are the same as those used in another procedure. Logo is able to keep all these details straight. This frees you to use input names

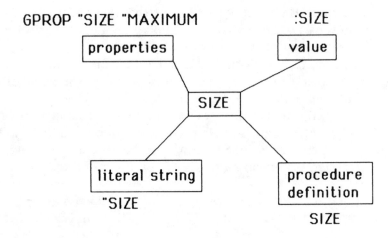

Figure A.2
The possible meanings of a Logo word

that are most relevant to the procedure at hand without worrying much about the context in which they might eventually be used.

The other way to create variables in Logo is to use the **MAKE** command. **MAKE** takes two inputs: a variable name and the value that is to be associated with that name. An example is

```
MAKE "SIZE 45
```

which assigns the value 45 to the word **SIZE**. Notice that you must use the quotation marks to tell Logo that you want 45 assigned to the literal word "**SIZE**.

When you use **MAKE** instead of inputs to create variables, the variables usually become permanent and global. The exception is when **MAKE** is used within a procedure to assign a value to a variable with the same name as an input to that procedure, as shown below:

```
TO EXAMPLE :NUMBER
IF :NUMBER < 0 [STOP]
PRINT :NUMBER
MAKE "NUMBER :NUMBER - 1
EXAMPLE :NUMBER
END
```

Because in this case **MAKE** is operating on a variable that is already local to that procedure, **MAKE** does not create a global variable.

When the **MAKE** command is used with a variable that is not an input to the current procedure, then the value becomes global. The variable's value is known to all the procedures in your workspace and is still accessible when the procedure finishes. This can become a problem if different procedures are creating global variables with the same name. Although Logo can keep track of numerous input variables of the same name, it cannot keep track of more than one global variable with a particular name. If you are writing procedures that create global variables, you must be careful not to use the same name in two different places, or the values may come into conflict.

Most of the projects in this book use inputs rather than the **MAKE** command to create variables. Occasionally it is necessary and desirable to have global variables, and in these situations the **MAKE** command is used. Other times global variables are created when their values are needed only temporarily and potential conflicts are few.

It is also possible to force a variable to be local to a procedure by using the command **LOCAL** (used occasionally in projects throughout the body of the book), as shown below:

```
TO FORCED.LOCAL
LOCAL "NAME
MAKE "NAME READLIST
PRINT FIRST :NAME
END
```

As a matter of general style, Logo programs should use inputs rather than the **MAKE** command to create variables, except where global variables are needed to make available a permanent copy of some variable to all the procedures in a workspace. This usage promotes modular programming projects and clean interfaces between procedures.

IF . . . THEN . . . ELSE STATEMENTS

Like most computer languages, Logo allows you to include, in your procedures, steps that are executed conditionally: that is, if something is true, then one thing is done; otherwise something else is done. An if . . . then . . . else statement takes the following form in Logo:

```
IF :X > 100 [PRINT "BIG] [PRINT "SMALL]
```

In this example, if the variable **X** has a value greater than 100, then Logo executes the instruction in the list delineated by the first set of brackets and prints the message **BIG**. If :**X** is not greater than 100, then Logo skips over the first list and executes the instruction in the second list, printing the message **SMALL**.

The general form for the conditional statement is

```
IF  predicate  [then clause]  [else clause]
```

The *predicate* is any Logo expression that yields **TRUE** or **FALSE**. Examples include

```
:X > 100
:NAME = "ICHABOD
:LASTNAME = :PATTERN
NUMBERP :INPUT
```

The *then clause* is a list of instructions that are executed if the predicate is **TRUE**. Most often this is a list of Logo primitives and procedures set off with square brackets, although sometimes the list is defined by a list-constructing primitive such as **LIST**, **SENTENCE**, or **FPUT** (see chapter 3 for more information on these primitives).

The *else clause* is a list of instructions that are executed if the predicate is **FALSE**. This list is optional. If it is not present and the predicate is **FALSE**, then the Logo interpreter continues execution with the next step in the procedure.

Very often in the procedures listed in this book, you see the then clause and the else clause listed on separate lines, as shown in

```
IF :YOURNAME = "JACK
    [PRINT [HELLO, JACK]]
    [PRINT [YOU'RE NOT JACK!]]
```

If you are using Apple Logo, you have to put the then clause and the else clause on the same line as the **IF** statement, that is, without hitting the <return> key.

In formal terms, **IF** is a Logo primitive that can take either two or three inputs. The first input is a predicate expression that evaluates to **TRUE** or **FALSE**. The second input is the list of instructions that are run if the predicate is **TRUE**. The optional third input is a list of instructions that are run if the predicate is **FALSE**.

REPETITION

Logo offers you several ways to make a section of instructions execute more than once. For example, if you want to print the word **HELLO** on the screen twenty-four times, you can use the Logo command **REPEAT**, as shown here:

```
REPEAT 24 [PRINT "HELLO]
```

REPEAT needs two inputs: the number of times that you want an action repeated and a list of the actions that are to be repeated.

This list of actions can be arbitrarily long, although if you find that you are putting more than three or four commands inside the brackets, it is probably best to define those actions as a procedure and then use the procedure inside the brackets:

```
TO BAD.STYLE
REPEAT 10 [PRINT "CONGRATULATIONS PRINT [] !
 PRINT [YOU ARE A BIG WINNER] PRINT [TODAY]]
END

TO BETTER.STYLE
REPEAT 10 [MESSAGE]
END

TO MESSAGE
PRINT [CONGRATULATIONS]
PRINT []
PRINT [YOU ARE A BIG WINNER]
PRINT [TODAY]
END
```

This same stylistic consideration can be applied to the lists that are used as then and else clauses with the primitive **IF**, as explained in the previous section. Generally, it is a good idea to package groups of instructions into procedures with meaningful names to make your programs easier to read and debug.

REPEAT is best suited to situations in which you know exactly how many times you want a particular action repeated. You can also use **REPEAT** even when you don't know the exact number of repetitions beforehand, by calculating the number at the time of execution, as shown in this example:

```
TO POLYGON :ANGLE
REPEAT 360 / :ANGLE [FD 40 RT :ANGLE]
END
```

This procedure draws polygons with any number of sides, depending on the angle that you give as input. The number of repetitions is determined by the expression **360 / :ANGLE**. If you type **POLYGON 60**, then the procedure draws a six-sided figure. **POLYGON 90** draws a four-sided figure. **POLYGON 85** draws a figure with only four sides, because the result of **360 / 85** is rounded down to the integer value.

You can see that using an expression that computes a number, such as **360 / :ANGLE**, in any spot where Logo expects to see a number works just as well as using an actual number. This is a very important concept in Logo programming.

RECURSION

The other main way to accomplish repetition in Logo is to use *recursion*. A recursive Logo procedure calls itself as one of its steps. The simplest example of recursion is that produced by a recursive call as the last step of a procedure; this is termed *tail recursion*. If you have three wishes and use the last wish to get three more wishes, you are practicing something analogous to tail recursion.

```
TO ENDLESS
PRINT "FOREVER
ENDLESS
END
```

When this procedure is executed, it first prints the word **FOREVER** and then goes on to the next step, which sends it back to the beginning to execute **ENDLESS** again. This process continues indefinitely, until you type <control> **G** to stop it. This same sort of iteration can be accomplished without recursion, by the two Logo primitives **GO** and **LABEL**:

```
TO ALSO.ENDLESS
LABEL "LOOP
PRINT "FOREVER
GO "LOOP
END
```

This technique is less desirable than recursion because it introduces the possibility of what is called *spaghetti logic* in programs (flow charts of programs that use **GO** and **LABEL** commands extensively tend to look like tangled masses of spaghetti). The examples in this book do not use the **GO** and **LABEL** command combination. Tail recursion is the control structure of choice in Logo when you want endless repetition.

You can also use tail recursion when you want to control the number of repetitions by examining the value of some variable at each cycle:

```
TO COUNTDOWN :NUMBER
IF :NUMBER < 0 [STOP]
PRINT :NUMBER
COUNTDOWN :NUMBER - 1
END
```

You use this procedure by typing something like **COUNTDOWN 100** or **COUNTDOWN 2001**. (If you feel like playing with this procedure, by the way, you can modify it so that it prints all the verses of "Ninety-nine Bottles of Beer on the Wall.")

The first step in **COUNTDOWN** examines the local input variable **:NUMBER** to see if it is less than 0 and stops the whole procedure if it is. If the number is not less than 0, then the number is printed. The next step is a recursive call to **COUNTDOWN**, except that now the expression **:NUMBER − 1** is used as the input. (Again, an expression that produces a number is just as good as the number itself.)

This same effect can be achieved without recursion with the following procedure:

```
TO COUNTDOWN2 :NUMBER
LABEL "LOOP
IF :NUMBER < 0 [STOP]
PRINT :NUMBER
MAKE "NUMBER :NUMBER - 1
GO "LOOP
END
```

This version is longer and less elegant than the original recursive solution, however.

A major argument against using recursion in programming has traditionally been that it is inefficient, making the computer do too much work to keep track of too much information. Normally, because each procedure, even a recursively called copy of an original procedure, keeps its own copies of input variables, the computer system must push variable values and return locations onto the system stack each time a recursive call is encountered. Logo is able to recognize tail recursion as simple iteration and bypass the normal recursive overhead, letting you use tail-recursive control structures without paying a performance penalty.

A second type of recursion involves a recursive call that is not the final step in the procedure. This is called *internal recursion*, and it is used extensively in the projects in the body of the book. Indeed, on one level the main topic of this book is simply how to use internal recursion to solve problems.

In internal recursion, a process that is going along is interrupted by another process that is actually just a variation of the original, and then the original is taken up again when the interruption is finished. Internal recursion leads to astonishingly elegant and compact solutions to certain problems, although it can be subtle and hard to understand at first.

Experimenting with the Logo procedures that are presented in the body of the book is a good way to experience and understand recursive problem solving.

PROCEDURES THAT OUTPUT

We have already mentioned several times that an expression that produces a number is just as good as a number in Logo. This is true for all data types: words, lists, and numbers. In other computer languages, you are often forced to pass the result of an expression into a temporary variable before using it with some other process. In Logo, results of expressions can always be used directly. One feature of Logo that encourages this practice is the **OUTPUT** command. With **OUTPUT**, you can write procedures that produce results usable directly by other primitives and procedures. For example, assume that you need to find out the fourth power of a number. You can type

```
:NUMBER * :NUMBER * :NUMBER * :NUMBER
```

every time you need that value, or you can define a short Logo procedure that takes the number as input and then **OUTPUT**s the fourth power of that number:

```
TO FOURTH.POWER :NUMBER
OUTPUT :NUMBER * :NUMBER * :NUMBER * :NUMBER
END
```

Now you can use **FOURTH.POWER 8** instead of **8 * 8 * 8 * 8**. This strategy works equally well for nonnumeric data:

```
TO MIDDLE.INITIAL :NAME
OUTPUT FIRST BUTFIRST :NAME
END
```

When a procedure reaches a step that has the **OUTPUT** command in it, the procedure halts, and the appropriate value is made available to the procedure that called the procedure containing the **OUTPUT** step. Using **OUTPUT**, you can write procedures that take in data as input and pass on modified copies of the data. Information can be passed from one procedure to another without the use of global variables. This technique is explained in detail in chapter 3 and utilized to a great extent in chapters

4 through 7. Suffice it to say here that **OUTPUT** is one of Logo's most important features and that you are encouraged to investigate its various uses further.

SUMMARY

This appendix is rather abstract. Logo is designed to be an experiential learning tool, and the formal overview presented here is thus best used as a reference.

Above all, do not be afraid to experiment and make mistakes with Logo. The system was designed to encourage exploratory learning. The best thing about Logo is not that it is fast or efficient but that it is particularly conducive to thinking about problem solving and to the exploration of interesting ideas.

APPENDIX B: WORKSPACE MANAGEMENT

The Workspace

Cutting Out the Deadwood

Packages

THE WORKSPACE

If you are used to programming in computer languages other than Logo, you may find Logo's method of memory allocation a bit confusing. In BASIC, for instance, you work with one program at a time. When you want to save your work to disk, the particular source code for that program is saved, but the current values of variables are lost.

In Logo, since there is no such thing as a program, you work with a concept known as the *workspace*. The workspace is filled with the definitions of procedures, the values of variables, and perhaps also property lists associated with words in the workspace. When you want to save your current work to disk, the entire content of the workspace is saved, including procedures, variables, and property lists.

The command **SAVE** is used to write the contents of the workspace onto a disk with a given file name. The file name does not have to be the same as the name of any of the procedures in the workspace, although you may find it helpful to give your files names that remind you what is in them.

It is possible to combine procedures from several different files on a disk by loading them all into the workspace at the same time. The combination workspace can then be saved into one file on the disk. This allows you to work on a big project in smaller sections, keeping the parts separate, and then finally combine the parts into an overall solution.

If two files that contain a procedure with the same name are loaded into the workspace, then the last one loaded is valid. This is true also for variables with the same name.

CUTTING OUT THE DEADWOOD

Because it is possible to have many procedures in the workspace at any time, it is common to accumulate unused procedures that are no longer part of the overall problem solution but continue to take up room in the workspace. These procedures should be removed with the **ERASE** command. Especially in microcomputers, memory is in short supply for Logo, so it is a good idea to cut out the deadwood now and then.

One trap that users fall into is illustrated by the following case. Say you load in a first file with several procedures, play with it for a while, and then decide to look at another file on the disk. You load in a second file, use its procedures, and perhaps modify them. Maybe you load in a third file and modify its procedures. Then you decide that you want to **SAVE** the modified third file. The problem is that if you use the **SAVE** command now, the procedures from all three files are saved, whereas you want the procedures from the third file only. To avoid creating files that are full of unwanted procedures, you must **ERASE** all the unwanted procedures from the workspace before using the **SAVE** command. You must also erase unwanted variables with the **ERN** command.

PACKAGES

Both Dr. Logo and Apple Logo allow procedures to be put into groups called *packages*. To package procedures, you simply use the command **PACKAGE**, giving it two inputs: the name of a package and a list of the procedures for that package. For instance, to put the three procedures **SQUARE**, **TRI**, and **RECTANGLE** into a package named **FIGURES**, you type

```
PACKAGE "FIGURES [SQUARE TRI RECTANGLE]
```

Once packaged, the procedures can be manipulated as a group by several commands. One of the handiest is **BURY**. When a package is buried, it is not saved to disk with the rest of the workspace by the **SAVE** command, and its procedures do not show up when you print out the names of all procedures with **POTS**. The buried procedures are, however, available to be run, just as if they weren't buried. If you want to bury the previously defined package **FIGURES**, you type

```
BURY "FIGURES
```

Later you can unbury it by typing

```
UNBURY "FIGURES
```

Burying packages is a good way to hide groups of tool procedures that you use on a day-to-day basis to aid programming but don't want to have saved in every file on your disk. You can keep the tool procedures in one disk file, load them in when you start to work, bury them, and then work on your other procedures. The buried tool procedures are there for you to use but do not clutter up the files of your other work in progress.

Packages also have many uses in conjunction with other Logo commands. Look into the documentation of your particular version of Logo for details.

APPENDIX C: ADDING PROPERTY LISTS TO TERRAPIN LOGO

The procedures listed here mimic the property-list primitives found in Dr. Logo and Apple Logo. Terrapin Logo for the Apple II series does not have the primitives to manage property lists. The procedures listed here, once typed or loaded in, allow you to work with all the examples in the body of the book that involve property lists. If you are using some other form of Logo and don't know if you have property-list primitives, there is an easy way to find out: try typing **TO PPS**. If your system complains to the effect that **PPS** is a primitive, then you do have property-list primitives and you can skip this appendix. Otherwise, type in the following procedures, some of which also appear in their Dr. Logo form in the discussion of list tools (chapter 4).

First, however, make sure you understand how properties are to be represented as data. As properties are defined, they are put into a list that is available to all procedures in the workspace. The contents of this list are also saved onto disk along with procedures when the workspace is saved with the **SAVE** command.

The properties are maintained in this list as sublists with three members: a word, the name of a property, and the value of the property. Thus, a workspace that has these two properties defined:

```
BOB'S FRIEND IS SAM
JILL'S DINNER IS GRILLED CHEESE
```

has those properties stored in a list that looks like this:

```
[[BOB FRIEND SAM] [JILL DINNER [GRILLED CHEESE]]]
```

Before we can put any properties into the list, we must initialize it:

```
MAKE "PROPERTIES []
```

Next we have to define a way to look at all the properties contained in **:PROPERTIES**. **PPS** calls **PPS.AUX** with **:PROPERTIES** as input. As you can probably see, **PPS** serves as a shell around **PPS.AUX**, which does the real work. **PPS.AUX** goes through the list of properties and feeds them one at a time to **PRETTYPRINT**. **PPS.AUX** uses the standard Logo technique of recursively passing over a list until the list is empty:

```
TO PPS
PPS.AUX :PROPERTIES
END

TO PPS.AUX :PROPLIST
IF :PROPLIST = [] THEN STOP
PRETTYPRINT FIRST :PROPLIST
PPS.AUX BUTFIRST :PROPLIST
END
```

Given the sample property list presented above, **PPS.AUX** bites off **[BOB FRIEND SAM]** and hands it to **PRETTYPRINT** on the first pass. **PRETTYPRINT** then takes **BOB** and adds an apostrophe (**CHAR 39**) and an "**S** to it, then takes **FRIEND**, then puts in "**IS**, then tacks on **SAM**, and finally prints the whole thing as

```
BOB'S FRIEND IS SAM
```

Note that **SENTENCE** in **PRETTYPRINT** has more than two inputs, so the inputs are all put within parentheses. **WORD**'s more than two inputs are also enclosed in parentheses:

```
TO PRETTYPRINT :PROPERTY
PRINT (SENTENCE (WORD FIRST :PROPERTY CHAR 39   !
 "S) FIRST BUTFIRST :PROPERTY "IS LAST :PROPERTY)
END
```

PPS allows you to see all the properties that have been defined in the workspace. If you want to see one particular property, say the **FRIEND** property of **BOB**, then you have to use **GPROP**. **GPROP** takes two inputs, a word and the name of a property, and then outputs the value of the named property. Notice that the value of the property is not automatically printed, as with **PPS**. With **GPROP**, the value of the property can be used for many purposes, as explained and demonstrated in the discussion of property lists (chapter 5).

Most of the difficult work in **GPROP** is done by **GPROP.AUX**. **GPROP** passes the word and property to **GPROP.AUX** along with the list of properties, **:PROPERTIES**. **GPROP.AUX** goes through the list until it finds a match for the word and property; then it outputs the entire matching entry. Looking for **JILL'S DINNER**, **GPROP.AUX** outputs **[JILL DINNER [GRILLED CHEESE]]**. **GPROP** then takes this list and outputs the last element of it, **[GRILLED CHEESE]**. In the event that **GPROP.AUX** does not find a match and thus outputs the empty list, trying to take the last element results in an error. To protect against this, **GPROP**, using **FPUT**, combines the output of **GPROP.AUX** with an empty list. This way, if there is no match, **GPROP** outputs the **LAST** of **[[ ]]**, which is **[ ]**. If there is a match, the output is the **LAST** of something like **[[ ] JILL DINNER [GRILLED CHEESE]]**, which is in this case, of course, **[GRILLED CHEESE]**:

```
TO GPROP :NAME :PROPERTY
OP LAST FPUT [] GPROP.AUX :NAME :PROPERTY :PROPER!
 TIES
END
```

```
TO GPROP.AUX :NAME :PROPERTY :PROPLIST
IF :PROPLIST = [] THEN OP []
IF ALLOF (FIRST FIRST :PROPLIST = :NAME)(FIRST!
 BUTFIRST FIRST :PROPLIST = :PROPERTY) THEN OP!
 FIRST :PROPLIST ELSE OP GPROP.AUX :NAME :PROP!
 ERTY BUTFIRST :PROPLIST
END
```

Now we can define a procedure to put a property into the property list. **PPROP** needs three inputs: a word, the name of a property, and the value of the property.

PPROP uses two other procedures to do all the dirty work.

REPLACE.OR.ADD, listed in its Terrapin Logo form at the end of this appendix, is a tool we developed in the discussion of list tools (chapter 4). It takes three inputs: an old item, a new item, and a list. It replaces the old item with the new item in the list. If the old item is not found, then it simply inserts the new item at the end of the list. In the procedure that follows, we see that **GPROP.AUX** is used to identify the old item by means of the input name and property, outputting **[]** if that property has not been defined before. The name, property, and value are combined by **LIST** (note that since there are more than two inputs, they are all enclosed within parentheses) and used as the new property. The list that is searched is the main property list, **:PROPERTIES**. For example, if you type

```
PPROP "BOB "FRIEND "JANET
```

then **REPLACE.OR.ADD** replaces **[BOB FRIEND SAM]**, which already exists in the list of properties, with **[BOB FRIEND JANET]**:

```
TO PPROP :NAME :PROPERTY :VALUE
MAKE "PROPERTIES REPLACE.OR.ADD (GPROP.AUX :NAME!
 :PROPERTY :PROPERTIES) (LIST :NAME :PROPERTY    !
 :VALUE) :PROPERTIES
END
```

Finally, you want to be able to remove a property from the property list with **REMPROP**. This procedure take two inputs, a word and a property, and removes that entry from the property list. This procedure uses **DELETE**, another tool developed in chapter 4 and listed in its Terrapin Logo form below, which removes an input item from a list. In this case, the item is described once again by **GPROP.AUX**. If you type **REMPROP "JILL "DINNER**, then **[JILL DINNER [GRILLED CHEESE]]** is removed from **:PROPERTIES**:

```
TO REMPROP :NAME :PROPERTY
MAKE "PROPERTIES DELETE (GPROP.AUX :NAME :PROPE!
 RTY :PROPERTIES) :PROPERTIES
END
```

The actions of **REPLACE.OR.ADD** and **DELETE** are explained fully in chapter 4, but they are listed here (in their Terrapin Logo form) for your convenience:

```
TO REPLACE.OR.ADD :OLD.ITEM :NEW.ITEM :LIST
IF :LIST = [] THEN OP (LIST :NEW.ITEM)
IF FIRST :LIST = :OLD.ITEM THEN OP FPUT :NEW.ITEM!
 :BUTFIRST :LIST
OP FPUT :FIRST :LIST (REPLACE.OR.ADD :OLD.ITEM    !
 :NEW.ITEM BUTFIRST :LIST)
END
```

```
TO DELETE :ITEM :LIST
IF :LIST = [] THEN OP :LIST
IF FIRST :LIST = :ITEM THEN OP BUTFIRST :LIST
OP FPUT FIRST :LIST (DELETE :ITEM BUTFIRST :LIST)
END
```

APPENDIX D: SUGGESTED READING

Abelson, Harold. *Apple Logo*. New York: McGraw-Hill, Byte Books, 1982.

The most complete introductory Logo book.

Abelson, Harold, and Andrea diSessa. *Turtle Geometry*. Cambridge, Mass.: MIT Press, 1981.

An immensely stimulating and challenging book on how turtle graphics can be used to investigate everything from population biology and coordinate geometry to the theory of general relativity.

Bridger, Mark. "Four Logos for the IBM PC." *Byte*, August 1984, pp. 287–301.

An excellent discussion of how Logo recognizes tail recursion as simple iteration (and, interestingly, how the Sieve of Eratosthenes can be represented in Logo).

Byte, LISP issue, August 1979.

A presentation of ideas that are very useful for guiding further learning with Logo, which is the godchild of LISP.

Byte, Logo issue, August 1982.

A wide selection of articles covering many different aspects of Logo and the Logo users' community.

Hofstadter, Douglas. *Gödel, Escher, Bach, An Eternal Golden Braid*. New York: Vintage Books, 1980.

A titanic and exhaustive book about recursion in art, music, and mathematics. Worth the long time it may take you to read. Written with a great sense of humor.

Thornburg, David. *Discovering Apple Logo*. Reading, Mass.: Addison Wesley, 1983.

A book that captures much of the elegance of Logo programming, presents a fine selection of problems, and is very clearly written. A gem.

Winston, Patrick, and Berthold Horn. *LISP*. Reading, Mass.: Addison Wesley, 1981.

An introductory book that develops in detail some of the more interesting advanced projects in LISP. Required reading if you want to learn LISP.

Wirth, Niklaus. *Algorithms + Data Structures = Programs*. Englewood Cliffs, N.J.: Prentice-Hall, 1976.

A book about Pascal, worth reading because of Wirth's central insight that the structure of data governs the structure of programs. Tersely written but full of wonderful ideas and strategies.

APPENDIX E: GLOSSARY OF SELECTED LOGO PRIMITIVES

This is a list of the primitives that are used in the projects in this book. It is certainly not a list of all Logo primitives. The primitives are listed in alphabetical order. Input requirements are listed with those primitives that take inputs. In such listings, the following conventions are used:

object can be a word, a number, a list, or an expression that outputs one of these.

predicate is an expression that evaluates to **TRUE** or **FALSE**.

< and > surround optional input (for example, the else clause in an **IF** statement).

(. . .) denotes a variable number of inputs. The default number of inputs is shown. If other than the default number of inputs is used, then the entire expression must be surrounded by parentheses. For example, to use **LIST** with more than two inputs, you must type **(LIST "FOO "BAR [THE ZOO])**.

.name(s) indicates the possibility of either one input or a list of inputs. For example, **ERASE** can take one procedure name, as in **ERASE "FOO**, or it can take a list of procedure names, as in **ERASE [FOO BAR BOO GOO]**.

AND *predicate predicate* **(. . .)**

Outputs the logical *and* value of its inputs.

ASCII *character*

Outputs the ASCII code number for *character*.

BACK *steps*

Makes the turtle move back the number of input *steps*.

BURY *package.name*

Causes the package named *package.name* to be buried.

BUTFIRST *object*

Outputs all but the first element of *object*.

BUTLAST *object*

Outputs all but the last element of *object*.

CLEARSCREEN

Clears the graphics screen and puts the turtle at the center, facing upward.

CLEARTEXT

Clears the current text screen and puts the cursor at the upper left corner of that screen.

COS *degrees*

Outputs the cosine of an angle measuring the input number of degrees.

DOT *coordinate.list*

Moves the turtle to the coordinates in the *coordinate.list*.

EMPTYP *object*

Outputs **TRUE** if *object* is the empty word or the empty list, **FALSE** otherwise.

END

Defines the end of a procedure definition started with **TO**.

EQUALP *object1 object2*

Outputs **TRUE** if *object1* is equal to *object2*, **FALSE** otherwise.

ERALL *<package.name(s)>*

When used without input, erases all unburied procedures and variables in the workspace. When used with optional input, erases all procedures and variables in the input package(s). If two or more *package.names* are input, they must be in a list.

ERASE *procedure.name(s)*

Erases the input *procedure.name(s)* from the workspace. If two or more *procedure.names* are input, they must be in a list.

ERN *variable.name(s)*

Erases the input *variable.name(s)* from the workspace. If two or more *variable.names* are input, they must be in a list.

ERNS *<package.name(s)>*

Erases all the global variables in the workspace. When used with optional *package.names*, erases only the variables in those packages. When two or more *package.names* are input, they must be in a list.

FALSE

Indicates a logical *false* value. Can be used in place of a predicate expression.

FENCE

Sets the screen edges as boundaries for turtle movement.

FIRST *object*

Outputs the first element of the input *object*.

FORWARD *steps*

Makes the turtle move forward the input number of *steps*.

FPUT *object list*

Outputs a modified *list* with *object* as its first element.

FULLSCREEN

Selects a full graphics screen with no text showing.

GO *label.name*

Causes execution of the line marked by **LABEL** *label.name* in the current procedure.

GPROP *name property.name*

Outputs the value of the *property.name* property for *name*.

HEADING

Outputs the current turtle heading in degrees.

HIDETURTLE

Keeps Logo from displaying the turtle while the turtle draws on the graphics screen. Speeds up graphics somewhat. Can be reversed with **SHOWTURTLE**.

IF *predicate list1* <*list2*>

Executes instructions in *list1* when *predicate* is **TRUE**.
Executes instructions in *list2*, which is optional, when *predicate* is **FALSE**.

ITEM *n object*

Outputs the *n*th element in *object*.

KEYP

Outputs **TRUE** if there is keyboard input waiting to be processed, **FALSE** otherwise.

LABEL *label.name*

Establishes a target for the **GO** command.

LAST *object*

Outputs the last element of *object*.

LEFT *degrees*

Makes the turtle pivot the input number of degrees to the left of its current heading.

LIST *object object* (. . .)

Outputs a list containing the input *objects*. Retains the outer brackets of the inputs. When used with more or less than two *objects*, the entire expression must be enclosed in parentheses. *See also* **SENTENCE**.

LISTP *object*

Outputs **TRUE** if *object* is a list, **FALSE** otherwise.

LOCAL *variable.name* (. . .)

Causes *variable.name* to be a local variable, known only within the current procedure. If two or more *variable.names* are input, the entire expression must be enclosed in parentheses.

LPUT *object list*

Outputs a modified *list* with *object* as the last element.

MAKE *variable.name object*

Assigns *object* to be the value of *variable.name*, such that :*variable.name* outputs *object*.

MEMBERP *object object*

Outputs **TRUE** if the first *object* is a member of the second *object*, **FALSE** otherwise.

NAMEP *object*

Outputs **TRUE** if *object* is a variable with an assigned value, **FALSE** otherwise.

NOT *predicate*

Outputs **TRUE** if *predicate* is **FALSE**, or outputs **FALSE** if *predicate* is **TRUE**.

NUMBERP *object*

Outputs **TRUE** if *object* is a number, **FALSE** otherwise.

OR *predicate predicate* (. . .)

Outputs the logical *or* value of its inputs.

OUTPUT *object*

Stops the current procedure and makes *object* available as the result of the procedure.

PACKAGE *package.name name(s)*

Puts the input procedure and variable *name(s)* into *package.name*. If two or more *names* are input, they must be in a list.

PENDOWN

Causes the turtle to draw lines on the screen as the turtle moves.

PENUP

Keeps the turtle from drawing lines on the screen as the turtle moves.

POS

Outputs a list containing the current *x* and *y* coordinates of the turtle.

POTS *<package.name(s)>*

Prints out the titles of the procedures in the workspace. When used with optional *package.names*, prints out the titles of procedures in those packages only. When two or more *package.names* are used, they must be in a list.

PPROP *name property.name object*

Assigns *object* as the value of the *property.name* property of *name*.

PPS *<package.name(s)>*

Prints all the properties in the workspace. If used with optional *package.names* input, prints out properties in those packages only. When two or more *package.names* are used, they must be in a list.

PRINT *object* (. . .)

Prints *object* to the current output device, stripping off the outer brackets of lists, and then performs a carriage return. If two or more *objects* are input, the entire expression must be enclosed in parentheses.

RANDOM *number*

Outputs an integer between 0 and the quantity *number* minus 1, inclusive.

READCHAR

Outputs a single character typed at the keyboard without waiting for the user to press <return>. *See also* **READLIST**.

READLIST

Outputs a list of keyboard input typed by the user. Input is accumulated until the user presses <return>. *See also* **READCHAR**.

REMAINDER *number divisor*

Outputs the integer remainder when *number* is divided by *divisor*.

REMPROP *name property.name*

Removes the input *property.name* property from the property list of *name*.

REPEAT *number instruction.list*

Repeats the commands in *instruction.list* the input *number* of times.

RIGHT *degrees*

Makes the turtle pivot the input number of degrees to the right of its current heading.

SAVE *file.name* <*package.name(s)*>

Writes the contents of the workspace to the file named *file.name* on disk. If used with optional *package.names*, saves only the contents of those packages. When two or more *package.names* are used, they must be in a list.

SENTENCE *object object* (. . .)

Outputs a list of its input *objects*. Strips the outer brackets of input lists. *Constrast with* **LIST**. When used with more or less than two *objects*, the entire expression must be enclosed in parentheses.

SETPOS *coordinate.list*

Moves the turtle to the position indicated by the input *coordinate.list*.

SETX *number*

Sets the turtle's *x* coordinate to the input *number*.

SETY *number*

Sets the turtle's *y* coordinate to the input *number*.

SHOW *object*

Prints *object* on the current output device, retaining the outer brackets of lists, and then performs a carriage return.

SIN *degrees*

Outputs the sine of an angle measuring the input number of degrees.

SPLITSCREEN

Sets the screen to display graphics in the upper region of the screen and four text lines (in Apple Logo) or five text lines (in Dr. Logo) at the bottom.

SQRT *number*

Outputs the square root of the input *number*.

STOP

Halts execution of the current procedure.

SUM *number number* (. . .)

Outputs the sum of its inputs. If less or more than two *numbers* are used as input, the entire expression must be enclosed in parentheses.

TEXTSCREEN

Sets the screen to display text only.

THING *variable.name*

Outputs the value of *variable.name*. Mimics the action of :*variable.name*.

THROW *name*

Continues execution at the line marked by **CATCH** *name*.

TO *procedure.name* <*inputs*>

Marks the beginning of a procedure definition with the name *procedure.name* and optional *inputs*.

TOPLEVEL

When used as a special name with **THROW**, halts the current procedure and returns to the Logo interpreter command prompt.

TRUE

Indicates a logical *true* value. Can be used in place of a predicate expression.

TYPE object (. . .)

Prints *object* to the current output device and does not then perform a carriage return. *Contrast with* **PRINT**. If two or more *objects* are input, the entire expression must be enclosed in parentheses.

UNBURY *package.name*

Reverses the action of **BURY** on the input *package.name*.

WAIT *number*

Causes a pause in the current procedure, the length of which is determined by multiplying *number* by 1/60 second.

WINDOW

Allows the turtle to draw off the edge of the screen without wrapping to the other side.

WORD *word word* (. . .)

Outputs a single word by concatenating its inputs. If less or more than two inputs are used, the entire expression must be enclosed in parentheses.

WORDP *object*

Outputs **TRUE** if *object* is a word, **FALSE** otherwise.

WRAP

Makes the turtle reappear on the opposite edge of the screen when it exceeds the screen boundary.

XCOR

Outputs the current *x* coordinate of the turtle.

YCOR

Outputs the current *y* coordinate of the turtle.

INDEX

More Computer Books from
Scott, Foresman and Company

Apple Writer Tutor
Learn to use the most popular word processing program for the Apple computer with this step-by-step tutorial. Includes instructions in plain English, a "Quick Start" section, advanced features, command reference sheets, and more. By Leshowitz. **$15.95**, 250 pages

The Apple WordStar Book
"This excellent tutorial/reference provides more detail than you'd need to start using WordStar. . . . Clearly explains Apple hardware modifications, WordStar commands, applications & hints."
—*Computer Book Review*. By Mar. **$17.95**, 277 pages

Commodore 64 Tutor for Home and School
Learn Logo, PILOT, and BASIC quickly and easily on the Commodore 64. Includes many examples, illustrations, and 3 full-length sprite and music programs. By Knott & Prochnow. **$15.95**, 224 pages

A BASIC Primer for the IBM Personal Computer
In a straightforward style laced with humor, the author provides dozens of examples that take the mystery out of BASIC programming. Includes end-of-chapter exercises and business applications. By Trivette. **$18.95**, 208 pages

Action Games for the Apple
Learn how to design your own computer games on the Apple II, IIe, II Plus, and IIc. The authors explain solid game design and programming techniques, and include 11 original games as examples. By Zimmerman & Zimmerman. **$8.95**, 200 pages, coming soon

To order,
contact your local bookstore or computer store, or send the order card to
Scott, Foresman and Company
Professional Publishing Group
1900 East Lake Avenue
Glenview, IL 60025

In Canada, contact
Macmillan of Canada
164 Commander Blvd.
Agincourt, Ontario
M1S 3C7

Order Form

Send me:

_____ Apple Writer Tutor, $15.95, 18012

_____ Apple WordStar Book, $17.95, 15992

_____ Commodore 64 Tutor for Home and School, $15.95, 18074

_____ BASIC Primer for the IBM PC, $18.95, 15997

_____ Action Games for the Apple, $8.95, 18091

☐ **Check here for a free catalog**

Please check method of payment:

☐ Check/Money Order   ☐ MasterCard   ☐ Visa

Amount Enclosed $_____

Credit Card No. _____

Expiration Date _____

Signature _____

Name (please print) _____

Address _____

City _____ State _____ Zip _____

Add applicable sales tax, plus 6% of Total for U.P.S.

Full payment must accompany your order. Offer good in U.S. only.

A18079